Keith Ward is Profes~~ional~~ Research
University of L~~~~ formerly Dean of Trinity ~~~~
Cambridge, P ~~~~ the ~~~~
at the Univer~~~~ of London, and Regius Professor of Di~~~~
the University of Oxford. He is a priest of the Church of England
and a fellow of the British Academy.

THE WORD OF GOD?

The Bible after modern scholarship

Keith Ward

First published in Great Britain in 2010

Society for Promoting Christian Knowledge
36 Causton Street
London SW1P 4ST

British Library Cataloguing-in-Publication Data
A catalogue record for this book is available from the British Library

ISBN 978–0–281–06211–9

1 3 5 7 9 10 8 6 4 2

Typeset by Graphicraft Ltd, Hong Kong
Printed in Great Britain by Ashford Colour Press

Produced on paper from sustainable forests

Contents

Contents

Part 4
THE NEW TESTAMENT

Part 5
THE DEVELOPMENT OF IDEAS IN THE BIBLE

Introduction: the Bible and modern scholarship

In 2004 I wrote a book called *What the Bible Really Teaches*. What I tried to do in that book was look at passages in the Bible which tend to be overlooked by fundamentalist Christians. I looked at passages about the return of Christ in glory, about salvation, about sin and grace, about the sacrifice of Jesus for our sins, about resurrection, about heaven and hell, and about the moral law.

I had myself been closely associated with fundamentalist Christians, and deeply moved by their faith and commitment. But as I looked at the biblical texts, I found increasingly that the Bible did not support their particular interpretation of Christianity – which was odd, because they claimed above all to be 'biblical Christians'.

What they were doing, I found, was to impose a rather narrow form of Calvinist and literalist doctrine on the texts, and sometimes actually twist the texts to give them a meaning quite different from their natural reading. This was not dishonest. They just honestly did not see that they had to force the texts to fit their doctrines, rather than the other way round.

I then tried to give an interpretation of the Bible just looking at the texts as they actually are, and found it very different from the fundamentalist interpretation. This again was very odd; for my friends typically claimed that other Christians (the vast majority of Christians, in fact) 'cherry-pick' the texts they like, and ignore others. Yet this is precisely what the fundamentalists were doing – and I set out to describe the texts they ignored or interpreted in a peculiar way in some detail.

I never claimed that my interpretation was *the* correct one. In fact my point was that the Bible can be interpreted in a number of ways, including Calvin's, which was more sophisticated than that

1

of many fundamentalists. The Bible contains many different sorts of teaching in its different letters, Gospels and prophetic writings. I argued that the fundamentalist claim to have the one correct interpretation of Scripture was almost certainly mistaken, and that other interpretations could be called 'biblical' with at least as much justification.

Though my book did propose a particular interpretation of the Bible, it left the texts more or less intact. It did not take into account the work of biblical scholars since the eighteenth century, who have asked critical questions about when the biblical books were written, by whom, for what purpose, and in what cultural and historical context.

However, thinking Christians, as well as those who simply want to know what sort of book the Bible is, now have to take such critical research into account. We cannot simply proceed on the assumption that the Bible was one book, written by God, carrying one coherent message. The Bible obviously consists of many books written over many centuries in at least three languages and in many different styles. Scholars who have devoted their lives to investigating these languages and their historical contexts have contributed enormously to our knowledge of the Bible.

Not all biblical scholars are Christians, or even believers in God. Some are very critical of Christian beliefs. But on the whole they have tried to give an honest and informed account of what historical methods and close analysis of linguistic forms can tell us about the Bible. Anyone who ignores their work, which has been going on for at least three hundred years, cannot any longer be regarded as competent to interpret the Bible.

For example, it was traditionally thought that Moses wrote the first five books of the Bible, the Pentateuch, including the account of his own death, which presumably he miraculously foresaw. Biblical scholars, by analysis of the text, have distinguished different strands or traditions with the Pentateuch, written by different authors in different styles and from different points of view, so that it is widely accepted among scholars that it was not all written by Moses.

It is true, of course, that biblical scholars are not infallible. They may be wrong. But if a majority of competent scholars who have spent their lives mastering ancient Hebrew language and history come to agree that the Pentateuch is an edited collection of different traditions, their opinion must be taken seriously.

If there is a consensus among scholars, we need to know what it is. If there are disagreements, we need to know what they are, and how strong the various arguments are. We cannot go on as though nothing had happened.

This present book, therefore, is about what happens to Christian belief, and to our reading of the Bible, if we take the work of biblical scholars seriously, but as always itself subject to criticism. It is about whether and how the Bible can be read as a sacred text after informed critical scholarship has done its work. And it is about how Christians can read and interpret the Bible if they pay attention to what biblical scholars say, but also want to read the Bible as Scripture, as an inspired text that is normative for Christian faith, as in some sense the word of God.

Some will think that informed critical scholarship has deprived the Bible of any credibility or authority, and that it is best relegated to a museum of ancient literature. But I argue that a critically informed Christian reading of the Bible can still treat it as the word of God, though only if it is interpreted with care and discrimination, and taken as a whole, so that all its individual passages are parts of a complex and many-layered unity that points beyond itself to the one true Word of God, the person of Jesus Christ. For Christians, the Bible is not the words of God. It is the witness to the Word, the eternal wisdom of God, who was embodied on this planet in Jesus. The Bible belongs not in a museum but in a church.

Part 1

THE NATURE OF BIBLICAL INSPIRATION

The Bible as a spiritual text

What is the Bible? It is still the world's best-selling book. Some people think it is written more or less literally by God, containing sets of moral instructions and wholly accurate accounts of human history, dictated direct from the creator in person. At the other extreme, some people think it is a set of nationalistic legends and ancient irrational taboos, which ought now to be regarded as obsolete.

It contains some wonderful passages of compassion and hope. Most of the Psalms, Isaiah chapters 40—55 (which scholars tend to call 'second Isaiah'), selected parts of the prophets, parts of the New Testament letters like 1 Corinthians 13 (the hymn to love), and the sermon on the mount (Matt. 5—7), are high points of literary and spiritual writing. But it also contains long lists of seemingly irrelevant laws (almost all the book of Leviticus – though that book does contain the sentence, 'Love your neighbour as yourself' (Lev. 19.18), which is arguably worth pages of boring instructions on bodily discharges and varieties of skin diseases). There are also some pretty gruesome passages on exterminating the Amalekites, calling on God to pour down fire and brimstone on one's enemies, and generally promising a coming day of wrath and terror for almost everybody (everybody else, that is).

So the Bible is a puzzling document, taken as the final guide to life by millions, yet denigrated by and offensive to many others. Perhaps the explanation of this fact is that the Bible is neither a book dictated by God nor just a set of outdated taboos and politically slanted histories. It is a very mixed set of documents by many different writers from many different times, which records the struggle of many people in one particular religious tradition to respond to their discernments of a transcendent spiritual power.

That power is spiritual, meaning that it is not material, not physical. It is more of the nature of mind and consciousness. But it is also transcendent, in that it is much greater than any finite mind. It is beyond the whole of space and time, though it is discerned through the events of space and time. And it is greater in value, in goodness and beauty, than anything in space and time. Many people feel an awareness of such a transcendent spiritual power. It can be a sense of presence, known through the beauty of a desert or of high mountains. It can be a sense of moral demand and obligation which encounters us with compelling force. It can be mediated through the impact of great art or music, through an inner sense of union with a higher self, or through our awareness of the awesome complexity of the physical world. Sometimes, but not always, people call this 'a sense of God', of a mind that has knowledge of the world and a purpose for it, and that has a causal influence in bringing about that purpose.

The patriarchs and prophets of the ancient Hebrew tradition interpreted their sense of transcendence in terms of the power of an active God. They saw that power in different ways – sometimes as a terrifying destructive force: 'Look, the storm of the LORD! Wrath has gone forth, a whirling tempest' (Jer. 23.19) – and sometimes as a compassionate saving and healing power: 'When the poor and needy seek water, and there is none, and their tongue is parched with thirst, I the LORD will . . . open rivers on the bare heights and fountains in the midst of the valleys' (Isa. 41.17–18) – and sometimes as a bit of both: 'He is like a refiner's fire and like fullers' soap; he will sit as a refiner and purifier of silver, and he will purify the descendants of Levi and refine them like gold and silver' (Mal. 3.2–3). What is quite distinctive about the Bible among the religious books of the world is that the dominant image of transcendence, of spirituality, that slowly develops in its pages is the image of a power that urges and helps humans to seek a moral goal in history even when such a thing seems humanly impossible to achieve: 'Let justice roll down like waters, and righteousness like an ever-flowing stream' (Amos 5.24).

The Bible is a story of repeated moral failure and desperate and sometimes misguided moral striving. The moral goal itself is sometimes seen in a very limited and exclusive way, as something that very few (the 'remnant') will ever attain. But at other times there is a hope that it can eventually be attained by all, despite human greed, pride and folly, with the help of some ultimately overwhelming divine power, the power of grace. It is a record of dreams and failures, ideals and nightmares, heroism and deceit. It is a human document, but it is a document of human interactions with what is believed to be a supreme spiritual power, placing before humans a supreme moral goal. And it is a document which expresses the very varied responses of humans to disclosures of that power, disclosures that have always been mediated through the events and experiences of individual human lives. The Bible is, in short, a spiritual text.

The Bible is, of course, mostly a Jewish book. The Hebrew Bible, the Old Testament, is a record composed by the prophets, historians, poets and lawyers of Israel. Today, interpreted with the aid of the Talmud and of the traditions of the Rabbis of Judaism, religious Jews still find in it an inspiration to seek justice and peace and the rule of goodness in a very unjust and violent world. I think everyone will admit that the search has always been morally ambiguous, mixed with nationalistic and vindictive motives, and it has never been wholly successful – Jerusalem today is hardly the 'city of peace' it was meant to be. Yet underlying it is a vision of transcendence as an ultimate spiritual reality that is itself supremely just and merciful, that calls the children of the covenant to embody such justice in history, and that promises that their moral struggles will not be in vain.

If you add the New Testament to this you get the Christian Bible. While owing almost everything to its Jewish roots, Christian faith puts the whole Bible in a different light by claiming that Jesus of Nazareth both negates and fulfils the Hebrew Bible prophecies and expectations. He negates them by becoming the origin of a new religious set of institutions, the Christian Church, no longer bound by Jewish law, centred on him as the decisive revelation of God. He fulfils them by taking the main strands of Jewish prophecy, law and wisdom, and bringing them to one focal point in his own person.

Christianity inherits all the ambiguities of Judaism. It can be interpreted in a restrictive, judgemental and negative way. Most of the world's population are doomed to hell. Only a few, those who consciously believe in Jesus, are the remnant who will receive eternal life. Urgent missionary efforts are needed to save a few believers from the terrible judgement that is coming upon the world.

But it can also be interpreted in a more universal, compassionate and positive way. There is judgement on human evil and corruption, but everyone without exception is offered a real possibility of forgiveness and eternal life. God wishes everyone to be 'saved' from evil and freed for a life of goodness and love. Missionary efforts exist to spread this 'good news' that all are offered eternal life with God, however miserable or imperfect their lives are. Divine forgiveness is freely offered to all who repent and turn to God. This is a positive gospel of new life, freedom and joy, and of hope for all, including those who may feel their lives are without point or purpose, and who are estranged from any sense of God.

I belong, and have always as a Christian belonged, to this second group. It includes Catholics, Protestants, Orthodox and Anglicans. The positive gospel is that, although humans live in a world dominated by hatred, greed and selfish pride, God has entered this world in Christ in order to forgive sin, free us from the power of self, and unite us to the divine life for ever. None who turn to him will be rejected. Even those who reject him God will not neglect, but will go to the furthest lengths to bring them into companionship with the divine life. That is the message of the cross – God goes to the uttermost lengths to draw us to God. And it is the message of the resurrection – God's love will not be defeated either by evil or by death.

This gospel is not founded on a book, not even on the Bible. It is founded on the liberating power of God, channelled through the presence of Christ in the Church. Yet for us to know what this power is, and what Christ is, we need the Bible.

The New Testament in its letters records the thoughts and experiences of some of the first disciples who responded to this good news of new life and joy in God. In the Gospels it presents memories of the life of Jesus, as that life has been reflected upon in the early Church, and as it has disclosed new facets of God's love to them. These documents, like the whole Bible, contain many different viewpoints, some of them rather petty or prejudiced on occasion, but all of them touched in some way by the grace of

Christ. We need to read them with discrimination, with an aware-ness of human partiality as well as of divine guidance ('inspira-tion'). We need to be helped to understand them with the aid of the best available biblical scholarship, and of the teachings of wise and saintly readers down the ages. If we do that, the Bible can become what it was meant to be, a record of human discernments of transcendence that has the purpose of evoking in us our own unique discernment of God. Since this discernment will be a response to the self-disclosure of God to us, we may rightly say that the Bible is 'the word of the Lord'. It is a text which has the power of conveying the presence and power of God to us. But we need to remember that, like all 'words' or texts, it carries many layers of meaning, negative as well as positive, and our understanding of it will largely depend upon our personal experience of the Christ to whom it must, for Christians, always point.

We should not expect, then, that the Bible is an inerrant text which provides totally correct information about God from start to finish. I see no reason to think that there are any such texts any-where in the world. All human knowledge is infected with error and limitations of understanding, and in my opinion religions are not exempt from this universal feature of human knowledge.

Even if some people think there is such an inerrant text, it is only their opinion that it is inerrant, and since they are human, their opinion is not inerrant. They may very well be wrong. So there is no escape from the fallibility of all human knowledge. If someone claims that the Bible is inerrant, we need to ask them, 'How do you know you are right? Might you not be mistaken about that? Do you really need to claim that a text contains no mistakes at all, before you can trust it and take it as a guide to your life?'

There is, after all, another interpretation. We can say that the Bible is a collection of human responses to what were felt to be en-counters with God in the history of Israel and in the dreams, visions and oracles of the prophets. Its various documents are mixtures of insight and prejudice, moving poetic evocations of transcendence and ugly expressions of human vindictiveness and petty-mindedness.

Overall, however, the Bible shows a series of developing insights into the nature of God as one creator of perfect beauty and perfection, who has a moral goal for the human world, and who relates to human lives with a mixture of categorical moral demand, forgiving compassion and the promise of ultimate hope for human fulfilment. It is one of the fullest and most complete accounts of the development of a human religious tradition over many centuries. It shows how contemporary religious believers have come to be where they are, and its general trajectory of thought suggests further directions of spiritual development.

We can speak of the Bible as inspired, in that we can see God at work influencing and guiding the minds of biblical historians, lawyers, priests, poets and prophets, so as to lead them to a cumulative tradition of insights into the nature and purpose of God, the ultimate spiritual reality. For Christians who believe this, the Bible is not the words of God, somehow by-passing the minds of men and women and dictating words direct from the divine mind. It is a unique witness to the gradually perceived purposes of God, which culminate in the prophetic teaching and life of Jesus, seen by Christians as a decisive and normative disclosure of the nature and purposes of supreme spirit.

Transcendent spiritual reality is spoken of in the Bible as a personal God, as appearing, calling, liberating, judging, forgiving, comforting, renewing, guiding and blessing. God is seen as relating actively with humans throughout their individual and social histories. This is a record of very varied discernments of a supreme spiritual transcendence and goodness which is not just a passive and impersonal ideal. It is apprehended as active in a personal way in the events of human lives. Such apprehensions are always perceived through the lens of human minds and thoughts. How prophets have seen God acting is partly a function of how they themselves relate to apprehensions of supreme goodness. In that sense the Bible is the record of one long tradition of human discernments of the divine.

For Christians, those discernments culminate in Jesus Christ. Many New Testament letters were written within a decade or so of the death of Jesus, and they give a vibrant account of the beliefs of the earliest disciples, who had either known Jesus personally or had been able to talk to those who remembered what Jesus had said and done. The letters and the Acts of the Apostles record the experience of the Holy Spirit in the early Church, bringing new life and hope, founded on the belief that Christ was risen and glorified, to the disciples. We trust their accounts if we accept that their new and living faith was indeed an authentic experience of God, which had come to them through the person of Jesus.

The Gospels are early records that contain remembered words and deeds of Jesus, and that witness to his death and resurrection. Many of those disciples were prepared to suffer and die for their beliefs, so it is entirely reasonable to trust their testimony to his teachings, death by crucifixion and appearances after death. Beginning from this point, it is Christ who must provide the key to the interpretation of the whole Bible. For Christians see the Old Testament as a gradual preparation for the decisive revelation of God in the person of Jesus, and its various texts must be interpreted in the light of Christ.

Even then, we must be aware that our personal discernment of Christ is imperfect, and so the spiritual task of reading the Bible sensitively and positively will never end. There is always more to learn, for the mystery of Christ will never be completely plumbed by any human agency of thought. Nevertheless, in our continual task of seeking greater understanding, the Bible is an essential guide to spiritual discernment, because it is in fact our only written guide to developing and recording the human discernment of the nature and purpose of God in Christ. In that sense, the Bible has final authority for Christians. But we should always be keenly aware that our own personal interpretation of the Bible will never be inerrant or completely adequate. God is revealed in and through the Bible, but our interpretation of the Bible, or even the one we learn from our friends, may leave much to be desired. That is why it is important to know about how the many diverse Christian churches, in many lands and at many different times, have interpreted the Bible for their own ages and cultures. That will help to put our own views in historical perspective, save us from undue arrogance and certainty, and give us a much broader understanding of the richness of the Christian gospel, which speaks in many forms to people of every age.

Is the Bible inerrant?

The Bible, regarded as a set of literal truths that are to be accepted just as they stand, says some very unpleasant things indeed. It says some things that are plainly and indisputably false, and some things that most people would regard as immoral. I will be talking about these in some detail later.

It will be a great help in reading the Bible as a spiritual text if we can admit that there are some errors and some limitations of perspective in it, that have been produced by the inability of the human writers to grasp the fullness of the love and mercy of the God revealed in Christ. Those errors and limitations do not undermine the witness of the Bible, taken as a whole and in the light of the life of Jesus, to the unlimited loving nature and purpose of God. Indeed, they can be a positive help in seeing how humans can grow, and must continue to grow, in understanding of God, how our understanding of God is never complete and final, and how God can use even the weak minds and hearts of men and women to convey a truth which is sufficient to unite us to God for ever.

We can very quickly see that the Bible is not inerrant, if we compare the accounts in different Gospels of Mary Magdalene and another woman or women coming to Jesus' tomb on the morning of the resurrection. Matthew's Gospel records that two women saw an angel descend from heaven, roll back the stone covering the entrance, and speak to the women. But the other three Gospels say that when Mary Magdalene went to the tomb, either alone (John), or with two other women (Mark), or with a whole group of women (Luke), they found that the stone had already been rolled away. They saw no angel descend from heaven, though Mark says that one angel was inside the tomb, Luke says that two were, and John says that two angels appeared later to Mary Magdalene. Then Matthew, Luke and John state that the women told the other disciples what they had seen, though Mark records that 'they said nothing to anyone, for they were afraid' (Mark 16.8).

I have chosen this event because the resurrection is of the very first importance to Christians. It is not just some peripheral and insignificant event; it is the very foundation of Christian faith. And the point is that the different Gospel accounts cannot all be correct. At least three of the accounts are indisputably false in some particular details. Whether you are a Christian or not, that is a fact you cannot escape. And of course if you are seriously concerned about the truth, you should not try to escape it. The conclusion is unavoidable: some Gospel accounts of the empty tomb are not literally accurate.

The only question is, what are we going to do about it? One course is to reject all the accounts as not trustworthy, and say that they are just made up long after the event. There was no empty tomb, and no vision of angels, at all. These are legends made up to support the reality of the resurrection appearances of Jesus. The theologian Rudolf Bultmann took this view, so it is not necessarily an anti-Christian view. But it does mean that there are legends, fictional stories, made up to make some sort of religious point, in the Bible.

However, there is another possibility. Human memories are notoriously unreliable, and second-hand accounts of events that someone else saw get embroidered and exaggerated very easily. If you ask a group of people who saw some event twenty years ago exactly what they saw, you will get quite a lot of variations in what they say. In fact, if you got exact agreement, you would immediately think that they had colluded in order to get their story straight. Small errors of memory are an indicator that there was a significant experience they all had, not a disproof that there was any such experience.

So a reasonably impartial historian might say that the different Gospels preserve different oral traditions that have developed in different ways, but may well preserve the personal testimonies of some women who recall having seen an empty tomb and having had a visionary experience of angelic presences.

That interpretation is, I think, a highly probable one. But there remains a major difficulty for many. The fact is that bodies do not normally disappear from tombs, and it is not at all certain that angels exist. These are extraordinary, miraculous events. Jesus' body simply disappeared, and there was a divine vision and a divine voice of some sort. If you are sure that such miracles cannot or do not occur, you will not accept the biblical account. On the other hand, if you think God could transform Jesus' physical body into a spiritual body, and that God could cause visions to occur, the literal accounts of the empty tomb will remain very striking.

Can we believe in biblical miracles?

How can we rationally decide whether or not miracles occur? A miracle is an extraordinary event, caused by God, which reveals the divine presence and purpose in a special way. A believer in God is committed to thinking that God, a purely spiritual power, is the cause of all things. So it is certainly possible that extraordinary events may occur which have a partly non-physical cause. Moreover, if there is a God with a purpose for the universe with which God wishes humans to co-operate, it is highly probable that God will bring humans to know what that purpose is, and how they are to co-operate with it. So it is probable that there will be extraordinary revelatory events. The prophetic visions and oracles of the prophetic tradition are such events. The Bible also records acts of liberation like the exodus, which have become definitive for development of the biblical idea of God. It is reasonable for a believer in God to think that such 'miraculous' events, awe-inspiring and not wholly accountable for in purely physical terms, are likely to occur. They will often occur through the mediation of prophets and those who are close to God. So it is especially likely that they will occur around the person of Jesus, who is the human embodiment of God.

All these considerations lead one to think that the miracles recorded in the Gospels may well have occurred, and are even rather likely to have occurred. On the other hand, we cannot just accept any claim to the occurrence of a miracle. We know that there is much deceit in spiritual matters. We know that human accounts of extraordinary events and people become embroidered with additional details, so that the lives of the saints are quickly surrounded with legendary elements. We know that sometimes metaphors get literalized, and that illustrative parables can be turned into allegedly historical accounts by pious imaginations. So we have good reason to think that many alleged miracles are largely products of human piety and imagination.

Since we have accepted that the biblical accounts are not iner-
rantly true, we might expect that, while miracles will occur in the
life of Jesus, there may be elements of hyperbole and literalization
in written and remembered accounts of them. This suggests that
it is quite reasonable to be rather agnostic about the literal truth
of many recorded miracles, but to accept that God was at work in
extraordinary ways in Jesus' life, so that there is an important core
of truth in the Gospel miracle stories.

There is an area of legitimate and inevitable uncertainty about
the interpretation of the biblical narratives. I am not proposing
to give the one correct interpretation. What the Gospel records
show is that early Christians believed Jesus to be a person in and
through whom God acted in extraordinary and spiritually profound ways. This belief was expressed partly in stories of miracles
surrounding the life of Jesus. That belief is important to Christian
faith. But I do not think it is necessary to accept that the miracles
occurred just as they are literally described in the Gospels.

I suggest that there is a range of acceptable opinions, from
fully literal acceptance to the view that these are partly legendary
accounts of the sort we often find in traditional stories of holy
men and women. The view we take will depend upon our more
general belief about the way in which God acts in the world. It
seems possible that God could act in extraordinary ways occa-
sionally without disrupting the general order of nature, and this
thought will encourage those who take the miracle stories literally.
On the other hand, we may ask why God does not act in these
ways more often, or why the point of some miracles seems so
trivial, or why miracles seem so rare today. And once we have
agreed that the Bible as a whole is not inerrant, we may accept that
over the years humans are very prone to exaggerate the unusual-
ness of events they have witnessed – medieval monasteries were
filled with improbable things like pieces of the true cross or even,
in the case of Reading Abbey, in England, a bottle of Mary's milk
and the foreskin of Jesus.

So a certain amount of scepticism is not unreasonable about
these matters. Literalists and sceptics will just have to live together,
agreeing that the important thing is that the records we have express

the spiritual claim that in Jesus God was disclosed in new and liberating ways.

I think it is only fair to state my own view, since though it is not one I would impose on others I believe it is well within the limits of reasonable Christian belief. My view, then, is that it is highly probable that Jesus performed extraordinary acts of healing. That is an important part of his message that God wills to heal and to save. I doubt if the healings were quite as instantaneous and total as some accounts claim, and I do not believe he exorcized demons. That is because I do not believe in demons, and think that these are exaggerated accounts of healings of mental illness, put in terms of what were then widely accepted, but false, beliefs about the causes of mental illness.

I doubt if the natural miracles, like turning water into wine – which are few in number (nine at most out of a recorded 35) – occurred, partly because they mostly seem like theological points (the water of the law turned into the new wine of the Spirit) turned into historical events, and partly because they conflict with Jesus' recorded refusal to produce any miraculous signs of his lordship (Mark 8.12: 'No sign will be given to this generation').

I doubt if the virgin birth occurred, since some texts seem to deny it (the Baptist did not know who Jesus was – 'I myself did not know him,' John 1.33 – which is odd if he really was his cousin, and Jesus' mother and brothers at one time tried to restrain him when people said he was mad – Mark 3.21 and 31 – which is odd if she knew his birth was unique, and if she had no other children), and it seems to rest on the misunderstanding that if Jesus was the 'Son of God' he could have no human father. However, being 'Son of God' is not a physical relationship, and so the incarnation of God in the person of Jesus is quite compatible with Jesus having a human father and mother.

I realize that in saying this I am distancing myself from ancient Church tradition, which very quickly developed devotion to the Virgin Mary as an important spiritual resource. Yet talk in the ancient creeds of God as 'Father', of Jesus as 'Son', and of Jesus as 'ascending into heaven' and 'sitting at God's right hand', is metaphorical, not literal. So it is not hard to see talk of 'the Blessed

Virgin' as a metaphorical expression of Mary's innocence, purity and total devotion to God, and to revere her as the uniquely chosen vessel for the birth of God incarnate.

Thus I think Christians could regard belief in the 'virgin birth' as having the status of a very early tradition, recorded in two Gospels, Matthew and Luke. But it is recorded in a story-like context, including stories of the wise men, shepherds and angels which many biblical scholars regard as unlikely to be literal. It is not, after all, theologically very important that Jesus had no human father. It has even been harmful in suggesting, quite falsely, to some that there is something impure about sexual congress, or that Jesus is the Son of God in some sort of physical sense, rather than that he is the incarnation of the Eternal Word. For these reasons, while I value devotion to Mary mother of God, I think the time has come to permit diversity of opinion in the Church as to whether the virginal conception of Jesus was a literal fact.

On the other hand, I believe the resurrection appearances did occur, since otherwise the Christian faith could hardly have arisen, and so the resurrection has an importance that the virgin birth does not. But some details, like Matthew's story of the dead rising from their tombs and walking around Jerusalem, seem to me legendary, if only because the dead are not confined to tombs after death.

What about the empty tomb and the angels? Since I believe that all humans will be resurrected in spiritual, not physical, bodies (1 Cor. 15.44), I think that Jesus was resurrected in a spiritual body. In that sense, it would not matter if his physical body disappeared or just decayed in the normal way. Yet the Gospels suggest that Jesus was able to manifest for short periods of time in a fully physical way (he ate fish, for instance – Luke 24.43 – and he bore the marks of the nails in his hands and side – John 20.25). In that case it would have been confusing if his physical body was still to be found in a tomb. I therefore find it quite believable that the physical body of Jesus in the tomb was instantaneously transfigured into a spiritual body, and left the tomb empty.

As for angels, it is undeniable that each of the Gospel accounts is different in detail, but all of them mention figures in white who declare that Jesus had risen. It is entirely intelligible that there should be created beings other than humans, and immaterial beings (which we may call angels) could well be among them. There are many accounts throughout the world of visions of spirits or non-human entities, and of voices or thoughts which seem to come from outside oneself. On the other hand, there are undoubtedly many hallucinations and delusions in human experience, and the medieval ranking of hierarchies of angels sometimes smacks of imaginative fantasizing of a rather uncontrolled kind.

A decision about the genuineness of such visions and auditions will depend on two main factors. Does belief in visionary experiences form part of an intelligible and coherent pattern of beliefs about the world? And is there any parallel to such experiences at the present time? Some will feel that angels play no causal role in our explanations of the world, and that claims to have such visions are too closely associated with mental illness to be taken seriously. But others will think that, given the existence of God, one might expect some visionary experiences which will be genuine manifestations of God, and which may take various finite forms. And they may feel that not all claims to visionary experience by apparently sane and intelligent people can be discounted.

Reasonable opinions may be expected to differ. The important point is the disclosure of divine nature and purpose in rare and astonishing human experiences. This may involve genuine apparitions and visions, or accounts of such apparitions may be literary ways of recording such moments of disclosure. My own inclination is to accept the authenticity of 'visions of angels', though with a tinge of uncertainty about what exactly their content was.

What I mean is that angels may not exist as specific and distinct individuals, for they may be finite forms of manifestations of the divine. That is, after all, how they are sometimes portrayed in the Old Testament, where there is often little distinction between an 'angel of the Lord' and the Lord in person (see Gen. 32.30, where Jacob wrestles with a man, and says, 'I have seen God face to face'). In other words, I accept the veracity of some strange and momentous human experiences of the divine, which may appear in various forms. But there are elements of the biblical accounts that I doubt

21

or am agnostic about, because they seem to conflict too radically with our present knowledge of natural processes, because various biblical accounts differ among themselves, and because we know that humans have a tendency to exaggerate and embroider events that have been important to them.

I have said that 'I doubt' rather than 'I disbelieve', because I am simply not sure that all the New Testament miracles occurred exactly as they are recorded, and I do not think that the occurrence of all of them is important to accepting Jesus as Messiah. But I do not doubt that they could have occurred, and so I prefer to be agnostic. To me the texts we have in the Gospels suggest that Jesus was perceived to be a man of extraordinary spiritual power, who did extraordinary things. Even so, the narratives of his life may show the same sort of hyperbolic exaggeration that we find in the hagiographies of many saints.

What is important for Christians, I think, is to believe that God did act to reveal and liberate in Jesus. Gospel accounts of these acts are shaped so that they might evoke in their hearers or readers the sort of disclosure that originally occurred to the disciples through Jesus. The accounts have been re-formulated in the light of subsequent Christian experiences in the infant Church. So for readers now the important task is to bring out the point of the miracle stories – and that point is to evoke disclosures of God and to see Jesus as the focal point of a new and amazing act of God in human history. This can be done even though the Scripture is not inerrant.

God does not provide one and only one consistent account of what actually happened in history, which cannot contain any errors of fact. In particular, biblical accounts of what Jesus did and said are based on more or less ordinary human memories, recorded, composed and interpreted to evoke in readers a sense of the presence of God in Jesus. That sense still has the power to transform our understanding of our world, and to bring to us the power of new life in the Spirit. That is the purpose of the biblical accounts, and that is the central clue to understanding what the Bible truly is – not a literally inerrant history-book, but a means of evoking a new spiritual perception of and a new way of living in the world.

Diversity in the Bible

There is a profound significance in the fact that in the four Gospels the Bible contains four different accounts of the same events that differ in detail. Each Gospel relates events from a unique viewpoint, placing them in different contexts of interpretation, even in different orders, and emphasizing different insights into the significance of the events. In the case of the resurrection narratives, Matthew gives the most dramatic account, with an angel rolling away the stone and astounding the guards, and with other bodies of the dead walking around Jerusalem. Mark's account is rather terse, and ends with the women keeping their experience to themselves. Luke gives a more literary version, with references to past words of Jesus. And John alone develops a story about Mary Magdalene seeing Jesus himself in the garden.

These differences reflect different interpretations of Jesus in each Gospel. Why should God reveal himself in this indirect way, through the collected memories and the personal interpretations, in different styles and narratives, of four different editors? One thing seems clear: these cannot be the words of God himself. They are the words of different persons, responding to what they know of traditions about Jesus. Those traditions themselves developed as they were passed on in various groups of disciples from original memories. The Bible contains human responses to revelations of God which have been experienced and interpreted and developed and reflected upon in different ways by different individuals and groups of disciples. In other words, there is no biblical revelation which is not already saturated with experience from a personal point of view, with interpretation and with many years of reflection included within it.

There seem to be six main stages in the genesis of the Gospel records as we have them. First, there are the original divinely caused events, often sayings or acts of Jesus. Second, there are

23

the original observations of these events, usually by small groups of people. Third are the memories of these observations, which seem subject to many of the normal vagaries of human memory. Fourth is the oral tradition which recounted and passed on these memories, and often included reflection or comment upon them. At this stage, many elements may have been added or elaborated. Fifth is the editing of various traditions into a narrative text, which expresses the characteristic interests and concerns of an editor. And sixth is the inclusion of the text into a canon of Scripture – a task performed by a committee, but perhaps reflecting some sort of consensus about the general reliability and spiritual importance of various texts.

There is a seventh stage, too, which is the later interpretation of the Scripture in a specific religious society. The Scripture might be translated in various ways, and different societies will interpret it in different ways – for example, whether people believe there is an intermediate state of Purgatory after death or not depends on differing interpretations of a range of biblical texts. Diversity again seems to be inevitable, and that may lead one to think that God must in some sense intend it. That is, Scripture invites a range of differing interpretations. This invitation is canonically enshrined in the four different Gospels, and is apparent in the many differing churches which exist in the Christian world.

The strange fact is that the more one church insists that it alone has the one true interpretation of Scripture, the more it evokes opposition from others who disagree. The most reasonable course is to accept the permissibility of a variety of interpretations. Of course they cannot all be correct. But there is no decisive way of certifying one as correct, and it seems to be more a matter of plausibility and spiritual efficacy than of certifiable truth.

We can put this fact of diversity in a positive way if we accept that it points to an inevitable partiality and limitedness in our own view, that needs complementing or even correcting by other views. It is a bit like the interpretation of a great literary work. Such a work invites diverse interpretations, bringing various sorts of insights. Some may be utterly implausible – if we think *Hamlet* is a comedy, for example, that is pretty implausible. But we would be glad that new voices can throw new light on literary works. We will have our own view, though it will be better if it is aware of other views and takes them into account. But we would be wrong to say that ours is the 'correct' view. What we are doing is bringing our personality and cultural tradition into conversation with a complex set of texts, which themselves contain many viewpoints. The uniqueness of our viewpoint is as important as our knowledge of other viewpoints. And of course some literary commentators are widely acknowledged to be more knowledgeable or insightful or exciting than others. In literature we do not look for the one true view. We look for creative and imaginative approaches which can deepen and enlarge our own understanding of human life, and enable us to see things in new and illuminating ways.

But isn't the Bible about truth rather than about literary appreciation?

Consider the question, 'What is the truth about Henry VIII?' There are some facts about Henry, there is no doubt about that. But many of those facts have not been observed by anyone, or they have been observed by people who later remember them differently. He broke with the Roman Catholic Church, that is a fact. But why? What was he trying to do? What were his own most basic beliefs and aims? Those things we cannot know for certain, since we only have later accounts from those who loved or hated him, and they interpret his actions very differently. We want to know what motivated him, what the meaning of his life was, why he acted as he did. Those things are seen differently, largely depending upon what our own attitudes and ideals are. The subjectivity of the observer cannot be eliminated. Indeed, it seems that the ideally dispassionate approach that the natural sciences require would be out of place in trying to understand another person. That is why a good novel or play will bring out many shifting facets of human character, but will still leave the innermost springs of human feelings, attitudes and intentions ambiguous or hidden, even from the agent who has them.

What we seek in literature is an imaginative sensitivity to the complexity of other persons and the way they see their world. Their inner reality remains hidden, and what we see of it depends on the way we approach it and the way in which it is expressed by a judicious selection of episodes from their lives, presented in a way that is intended to convey some specific points.

So it is with the Bible. The Bible is, overall, a narrative of the history of God, seen from a number of perspectives that respond to God in many different ways over many centuries. In the Christian Bible there are histories, law-codes, proverbs, hymns, stories, prophecies, records of visions, letters and the four Gospels. The books of the Hebrew Bible have been used by the Jews to inspire and sustain a rich tradition of debate, discussion and imaginative re-interpretation (found in parts of the Talmud). The books of the Hebrew Bible remain important to Christians, though Christians no longer have a tradition of Rabbinic interpretation, and re-interpret the books in the light of what they regard as a supreme revelation of God in Jesus the Messiah, or Christ.

The Gospels are edited collections of memories of Jesus, seen by Christians as a decisive disclosure of God, bringing the whole Jewish tradition to a sort of culminating revelation. The Gospels are already theological works, since each presents a distinctive interpretation of the meaning of Jesus' life and words. They do so in narrative form, the interpretation being largely given by the selection and juxtaposition of the materials. The other main part of the New Testament is a number of letters written to very early churches (often pre-dating the Gospels). These letters are obviously not the actual dictated words of God, addressed to humanity in general. They are written to specific groups in response to specific problems, and from various points of view. They are interpretations of the 'basic gospel' of Jesus' death 'for our sins', his resurrection, and his final appearing in glory. They are regarded as 'inspired', because they came to be regarded as profound insights into the meaning of Jesus' life, written very early in the history of the Church by leading teachers in the Church, and accepted as an authoritative basis of Christian discipleship.

They are authoritative in much the same sense that the teachings of Augustine or Aquinas or the Pope may be authoritative, though they possess the advantage that they are nearer the source of Christian faith in time – although it is true that later reflection on past events in the light of subsequent history can also bring out meanings that were not perceived at first. If we think that God was over many centuries guiding the prophets of the Hebrew tradition to fuller insights into the divine nature and purpose, then the prophetic message of Jesus, and the insights that his life, death and resurrection prompted among his disciples, will be of crucial significance in religious history. It will be wholly reasonable to think that God inspired the New Testament authors and editors in such a way that a new paradigm revelation was definitively recorded and witnessed to in their writings.

Not everything they say is inerrant. But it is reasonable to believe that the main outlines are definitive for all future developments in Christian thought and practice, and it is by God's will that they are preserved in Scripture. Each part of the letters has something valuable to express – even if sometimes, as with parts of the Old Testament, it may express how limited even the most faithful human perceptions are.

The existence of the New Testament letters confirms a view of divine revelation as God's co-operative guidance of many diverse human minds, as they reflect on experiences of God that have occurred around the person of Jesus or in the communities founded in his name. They are the authoritative founding documents of the Church. But we still need to read them with discernment, distinguishing their central important truths (what Jesus' death, resurrection and glorification means for our human world and for the cosmos) from cultural or psychological conventions or the very limited scientific knowledge of their day, and re-interpreting their insights in the very different circumstances in which we may now live.

What does inspiration mean?

Christians usually believe that the Bible is inspired by the Spirit of God. The biblical view of inspiration is quite different from the view that some other religions take. Biblical inspiration cannot be divine dictation, as it is said to be in the Jewish Torah, the Muslim Qur'an or the Indian Veda. What then is it? I have suggested that we might best see it as a sort of divine guidance, a raising of the mind and heart to a greater sensitivity to divine presence and purpose, with an increase in the ability to express in memorable ways the insights such sensitivity brings. Such influence does not, as has been demonstrated, eliminate all errors or defects of memory. It does not overrule the unique personal styles and interests of human persons. But it does shape them to a deeper insight and more meaningful form of expression.

This is a fairly common sense of 'inspiration' in human life. The speech of an orator may be called 'inspired' when it gives a new insight or produces courage and devotion in its hearers. This everyday sense of inspiration need not have God as its source. It may be that orators like Adolf Hitler were inspired, but not by God. Biblical inspiration is distinctive because Christians believe it is caused by God, and in some fashion it conveys what God wishes to convey. Through his inspiring of human minds, God wishes to convey something of importance for human fulfilment and salvation.

In the case of the empty tomb, we may think that God did act directly and miraculously to transform Jesus' physical body into a spiritual body, and perhaps to cause an angelic vision to occur – though some Christians would think that such events are not important to belief in the resurrection, and may not have literally occurred. There follows a long and complex process of inspiration. Even if such events occurred, God must ensure that someone observed the tomb and the vision, or there would be no revelation at all. God must ensure that the observers do not completely forget or misinterpret what they have seen – though there is apparently room for memory-vagueness and literary elaboration. God must ensure that such memories get passed on in an oral tradition – though again there will be differing traditions, so that it is the general or core elements that are preserved rather than the details. God must ensure that the traditions are incorporated into a canonical or authoritative body of teaching (a Scripture) – a Scripture that will include memory differences and diverse interpretations of their meaning or spiritual significance.

I think the most plausible account of this long and complex process of inspiration is that God does not act unilaterally to put thoughts or words into people's minds. Rather, God co-operates with human minds, influencing memories and thoughts but not overruling them or taking them over like an alien mental controller.

Once we have accepted that there are differing accounts in Scripture, and that not all of them are strictly accurate, it will be reasonable to allow more radical accounts, which see more elaborations and legendary accretions in Scripture, to live alongside more conservative accounts, which are happy to accept that empty tombs and visions can and are likely to occur. We will not be automatically committed to more radical views. That may depend upon more general factors like whether we think physical miracles occur, and what the physical limits on such miraculous events may be. It will be natural for us to accept what seems more likely to us, given our general evaluation of probabilities, and our sense of what physical events are required for full belief in the resurrection of Jesus. I would expect differences of judgement on such issues among those who accept the fact of Jesus' resurrection, and I would not be inclined to draw a hard and clear line that defines what beliefs are strictly required of a Christian in these areas.

The effect of such divine influence will partly depend on the receptivity of the human mind to it. If that is so, there may be certain blocks or deficiencies of vision that impede a full understanding of what God wishes to communicate. We might expect to find not only an expression of personal insights and concerns, but also some failures to understand God's nature and purposes, because such fuller understanding would be completely alien to the mind of the observer or writer.

That is one reason why diversity might be important. The deficiency or 'one-sidedness' of some accounts might be counter-balanced by complementary insights in other accounts. In the case of the Gospels, the concentration on Jesus' humanity in Mark is complemented by an emphasis on Jesus' divinity in John. Read separately, these Gospels give very different views of Jesus' relation to God. Taken together, they do not provide one wholly harmonious account. They give two perspectives on Jesus, and invite the hearer to form a personal perspective, given that such a diversity of inter-pretations is natural and proper to human life.

The Bible, then, contains some errors, and also contains limita-tions of insight and understanding. It is a human document, or rather a set of documents compiled over hundreds of years by very different writers at very different stages of history, from the Bronze Age to the Classical era. But Christians take it as inspired by God, in the sense that, taken as a whole and read sensitively, it conveys the message of salvation and of God's nature and purposes that God has wished to see communicated through this religious tradition. God has overseen that process of communica-tion, but has not overruled the diverse and developing human perspectives that have gone to form it over a long period of time.

This could be called a 'co-operative guidance' model of inspira-tion. God leads some humans, living within one social tradition with a long history, gradually towards greater insight into the divine purpose. But some perspectives need correcting or placing within a wider context, and none are guaranteed to be immune from misuse or misinterpretation.

The question that all those with a strong sense of biblical authority ask is: if so many parts of the Bible are in error, or reflect human responses to divine actions, how can I trust any of it or suppose that it relates what God's purposes truly are?

This is not a question that would seem reasonable with regard to any other literary or scientific or historical text. We might trust a historical account of the Battle of Waterloo, while expecting that some details may be inaccurate or expressed in a partisan way.

We know that people make mistakes and have limited perspectives. That does not stop us trusting what they say on matters they have researched carefully. A Dostoevsky novel may give great insights into human life, without its views being wholly acceptable. A scientific treatise by a reputable expert may turn out to be mistaken, but we would be well advised to accept it as the best account we have on a given subject, and it would be silly to think that it is entirely mistaken from start to finish.

So why should we expect a religious text to be exempt from such common human errors? What distinguishes the Bible is that it is about the acts of God in history – acts of saving from disaster, or inspiring poets and artists, or causing visions, auditions and miracles to occur. We may say that we would not know how God has acted unless these accounts of them are preserved from all error. That is like saying we would not know who won the Battle of Waterloo unless some historian was preserved from error. That is both false and unrealistic. Some historical claims are so well attested, on such reliable authority, that we do not doubt them, even if we cannot test them ourselves. We do not need infallibility; we need trustworthy witnesses of well-attested events.

When events are recorded in the Bible, that does not prove that they actually happened. It would not help to say that the Bible is inerrant, for we cannot know that until we know if the events it records happened. What, then, makes the biblical accounts of Jesus believable? In the first place, the fact that reliable witnesses, who have much to lose by their claims, testify that they have personally witnessed the life of Jesus over a fairly long period of time, that he appeared to them to have immense wisdom and authority, and that they saw him die and appear after death. In the second place, a general belief that there is a God will raise the probability that God has decisively revealed the divine nature and purpose in an extraordinary way. In the third place, the Old Testament prophets looked forward to a decisive disclosure of God in a Jewish Messianic figure, and Jesus is claimed to be that figure. In the fourth place, these accounts have been used to form the devotional life of a church, and they have conveyed a sense of Jesus as a living and transforming spiritual presence to thousands of devotees who meditated on them. They speak of God revealed in the person of Jesus, and they convey such a revelation to their hearers on many occasions.

So we start with the Gospel accounts of the life of Jesus. These have been collected and edited from the oral traditions of different groups of disciples, and they are based on memories of those who knew Jesus personally. We have every reason to think that they are broadly accurate, though they will probably contain some obscure or inaccurately remembered or embroidered material, and quite a lot of personal selection and interpretation, especially by the editor.

The accounts have been written down for a purpose, and that is to present Jesus as a living mediator of God. They are not just biographies. They are like collections of mini-sermons to bring readers into the presence of their Lord. They have a devotional purpose, and we misread them if we do not see that. But devotion takes many forms, depending on our own ideals and values, and so the four Gospels express different devotional attitudes. The existence of four Gospels shows that all those attitudes are appropriate for Christian disciples.

The Gospels are inspired – that is, the whole process of remembering, selecting, writing down and inclusion in the Bible is guided, Christians believe, by the Spirit. Human memories and perspectives remain, but God uses them to create new insights into God's nature and purposes, and to shape our minds on the mind of Christ.

In reading Gospel passages, we must seek such insights from God. But we should also be aware of our own limited understanding, and of the fact that there may be great limitations in the written texts, as the disciples, the churches that preserved their memories, and the editors who wrote them down, put some of their own prejudices and hang-ups into the text.

The Bible is not primarily a set of true propositions to which we are asked to give theoretical assent, even though many fairly straightforward truth-claims are made in the Bible. It is primarily the sacred text of a religious community, a community that relates to God, the primal reality, in worship and reverence. A sacred text is not information about otherwise unknown facts. It is like a sacrament, an outward and visible sign of an inward and spiritual meaning. Its information content is often indirect and mysterious, metaphorical and allusive. Moreover, it must be taken holistically and in a context of worship. Individual parts cannot be taken out of context, for their meaning depends upon the wider set of texts of which they are part. And the whole set of texts, the Bible itself, is properly read as part of an act of divine worship, of glorifying God.

To be a biblical Christian is not primarily to accept the truth of lots of unusual facts. It is to respond passionately to a God who reveals the divine reality through events of personal significance, but in a way that can only be rightly discerned, believers would say, by minds and hearts open to transcendence. Reading the Bible in the light of faith in the unlimited love of God shown in Jesus Christ is one way of allowing God to reveal the divine presence to us. Such a revelation cannot be identified with simply accepting that whatever the Bible says is true. The text must be used in such a way that it allows God to address us personally, as we read it in the context of the Church's worship and of the Christ-illumined key to interpreting each part of the Bible.

Part 2

THE OLD TESTAMENT

Reading the Old Testament

———◆———

The Bible is a set of richly metaphorical texts which present a theistic interpretation of history, or history seen as the arena of divine actions. It records discernments of God, the transcendent spiritual reality underlying the events of history, and it does so in order to evoke discernments of God in those who hear or read the narratives.

The history is largely derived from remembered oral traditions, which have been enhanced and elaborated with mythical and legendary elements to magnify the glory of the God of Israel, and tend to overlook occasions when that glory has been less than obvious (when Israel has been defeated in war, for example). The biblical historians include different and conflicting traditions, as in the books of Kings and Chronicles, which present the same events in very different ways. The narratives include a strong theological bias – so that after Israel and Judah split apart, the historians of the southern kingdom of Judah represented all the kings of Israel as corrupt and evil. Less biased historians would say that in fact some of them, like Jeroboam II of Israel, established fairly secure and successful kingdoms. But that did not suit the aim of the Chroniclers, who wished to defend the Davidic dynasty of Judah and decry the achievements of the northern kingdom of Israel.

Sensitive accounts of these matters can be found in many books by Old Testament scholars. One I like is *The Living World of the Old Testament*, by Bernhard Anderson (Longman, London, 1975), though there are many others. Good commentaries on individual books in the Bible include the Anchor commentaries, which represent a consensus among leading biblical scholars, and the *Oxford Bible Commentary* (Oxford University Press, Oxford, 2001), edited by John Barton and John Muddiman, which also includes articles by scholars from most main Christian churches.

Most scholars agree that the biblical history is itself diverse, and is very different from the account that a secular historian might give. There is no reason to be unduly sceptical – the accounts of the reign of David, for example, are among the most reliable historical accounts we have of that antiquity. But one should not pretend that the best Old Testament scholars all think that we have a perfectly accurate history in these texts. On the contrary, they mostly think that the accounts have been simplified, schematized and elaborated to provide a particular view (in fact, two or three different views, laid alongside one another) – in hindsight and pious memory – of how God was helping and judging the Hebrew tribes at key points in their history.

What is distinctive about the Bible, in comparison with other Near Eastern religious texts of a similar period, is its emphasis on history as the arena for discernments of God. The God who is thus discerned is a morally demanding God, requiring and rewarding the pursuit of justice (symbolized by giving the Torah to Moses) and punishing injustice. God calls the people of the 12 tribes to a specific vocation in the world, liberates them from slavery to enable them to follow that vocation, of being 'the priests of the LORD' (Isa. 61.6), and promises that his purpose of establishing a kingdom of justice and peace will be realized.

These great themes of the Bible doubtless developed over centuries, in ways that were seldom clear-cut and unambiguous, and were represented in new and ever more elaborated ways many times. But in the final edited text they are represented as highly stylized key episodes in history, when God appears and speaks in clear, definite and wonderful ways. Thus God speaks directly with Moses, even writing the laws with a divine hand on clay tablets. God appears in a pillar of cloud by day and a pillar of fire by night to lead the Israelites miraculously through the Sea of Reeds, liberating the people from slavery and destroying all the pursuing Egyptians. God speaks with Abraham and makes a covenant with his descendants for all time. God directly punishes the wickedness of Israel and directly rewards obedience to the Torah.

These are not records of what exactly happened. They are cultic narratives which represent, in episodic story form, the demand, liberating power, calling, moral judgement and promise which the Hebrew prophets gradually came to discern as they worshipped their God in the many vicissitudes and ambiguous processes of their history.

Thus the biblical narratives of history are not *evidence* for the truth of a religious view. They are *dramatic presentations* of a current religious view read back into history. At no stage in the development of the Hebrew Bible is the current religious view entirely correct, fully adequate or without nationalistic or moral limitations. Thus when Moses calls for the complete extermination of the Canaanites (Deut. 20.16), this is not an account of what God or Moses actually said. It is an excessively vindictive and ultra-nationalistic expression of the frustration and anger of a much later writer, who wishes that all the Canaanites, in his own day causing so much conflict in his country, had been exterminated long ago. So the writer reads the extermination command ('the Ban') back into Moses' speeches. That command had never existed and had never been carried out – thank goodness! It is wishful thinking by a very intolerant and zealous writer.

What lessons does it have for us? The main lesson is that religious zeal can go badly wrong. Instead of leading, as it should, to the selfless service of others, it can lead to a desire for the extermination of the so-called 'enemies of God'. This desire is present in the Bible, just as is the expressed wish for the killing of Babylonian babies (Ps. 137.9 – 'happy shall they be who take your little ones and dash them against the rock'). People who have such desires have a lot to learn about God. They are completely wrong about what God wants and commands. But that is part of the development of our ideas about God and about justice, and it must be acknowledged – and then disavowed.

It would be grossly immoral to take these commands as binding on us, or to think that at some time they were actually good. We have to see them as early and perverse stages in the development of better insights into the nature of God. Those better insights are in the Bible, and for Christians they are mainly found in the teachings of Jesus, the fulfilment of the prophetic tradition. In the light of these teachings, we can learn to discriminate between different parts of the Bible. We can say that the writer of the Deuteronomic laws was right about there being one creator God who liberates the Hebrew tribes and calls them to pursue the moral goal of justice. But he was wrong about what justice is and about how we should treat those who disagree with us. We should love our enemies and aim at the well-being of all – but it took many centuries for the biblical writers to see that clearly. Christians who still believe that we should bomb our enemies and reduce them to penury have not seen that Jesus' message superseded much of the teaching of the Old Testament.

The question, 'Are the historical narratives of the Bible true or false as they stand?' is natural but misleading. They are dramatic presentations of religious attitudes, projected onto the past, elaborating core discernments of God that cannot now be recovered in literal detail. These dramatic presentations are meant to be rehearsed in thought by their hearers. Repeating these paradigmatic episodes of their tradition, hearers are to renew in themselves a sense of the demand, calling, judgement, promise and power of their God. But they are to do so in the knowledge that the ancient narratives must take a new form in their lives, in conditions of life which are very different, and in the light of later qualifications and re-interpretations that are found in later biblical texts. These episodes are recited rituals, whose repetition is intended to renew devotion to the God whose presence they symbolize.

The ritual narratives are founded in history, and in discernments of a historically active God who has a moral goal for the world and a moral vocation for Israel. The original history is never exactly recoverable, and what is primary is the symbolic efficacy of the narratives in a present religious community. Is there a transcendent reality, a God with this character, who can be known and worshipped in this tradition? Can these ritual narratives, now so ancient in origin, still carry the power to evoke a sense of God, despite all their limitations of perspective and understanding?

Prophecy provides the best example of the projection of historical narratives onto a cosmic scale, when it speaks of contemporaneous political dangers for Israel, for example, in terms of judgement on the world (the 'Day of the Lord'), of the darkening of the powers of the heavens, and of a Davidic king who will return to lead a faithful remnant into a renewed world and to the true worship of God. These prophetic symbols were, Christians think, fulfilled in Jesus, and so they are tremendously important as pointers to future disclosures of God. But they were fulfilled in quite new and unexpected ways – for Jesus did not rule as a king in a Jerusalem palace, but was crucified on a hill outside the city walls. So, for Christians, the Hebrew Bible anticipates and points to fuller discernments of God, but often in very obscure and imperfect ways.

Christians can accept the Bible as a record of developing and diverse human discernments of God, gradually being developed within a community of worship and prayer that culminates in a paradigmatic disclosure of God in the person of Jesus. We should trust the Bible because it points us to Christ, and Christ is known in the community of the Church as the living presence and power of God which enters into and transforms our lives. From that point on, Christ becomes the test of biblical truth. If we bear that firmly in mind, we can say that the formation of the Bible is inspired by God, in that God gradually led human minds to new perceptions that were, unknown to them, to lead to the culminating revelation of God in Jesus Christ.

If there were no imperfections in the Bible, it would not be a pointer to a greater fulfilment in Christ. If there were no diversity in the Bible, it would not represent the richness and variety of human encounters with God in Christ. If there were no development in the Bible, Jesus could not be seen as a new and decisive revelation of God. If there were no truth in the Bible, we would not know what Jesus was and taught. It is through the Bible, as it is understood in the believing community of the Church, that we come to a living consciousness of God in Christ. Because of that, the Bible has an irreplaceable authority for the Church. But Christ stands over the Bible, as the living Spirit stands over the written law, and he provides the standard by which each stage of biblical revelation is to be allocated to its proper place in the long and chequered history of the reception of divine self-disclosure by the prophets of the Hebrews.

The prophets

The prophetic tradition in Israel arose as part of the turbulent history of the 12 tribes. In the Hebrew Bible there are three 'major prophets' – Isaiah, Jeremiah and Ezekiel – and 12 'minor prophets' whose words and deeds have been recorded. Biblical scholars mostly agree that few, if any, of these books contain the actual words of historical prophets. The book of the prophet Isaiah, for example, is usually divided by scholars into three or four different books, edited by different writers at different times of history. But there were historical prophets, and what is attributed to them is probably representative of what they said and did.

Prophecy probably began as an institution with the early monarchy. In 1 Samuel 9.9 it is recorded that prophets used to be called 'seers', people alleged to have powers of clairvoyance. There were also bands of prophets (*nabi*) who fell into ecstatic frenzies under the influence of music and dancing, and uttered cryptic oracles. Later prophets were partly advisers to the royal court, and partly individuals, like Amos, who were said to be directly inspired by God to utter words of judgement on evil and promise of deliverance from evil.

The prophets Amos, Hosea, Micah and first Isaiah belong to the eighth century BC, when Assyria was about to conquer Israel and threatened the southern kingdom of Judah. Nahum, Zephaniah, Habakkuk and Jeremiah lived in Judah in the seventh and sixth centuries BC, before the Babylonian invasion of that small kingdom. Ezekiel and deutero (second) Isaiah were prophets of the exile in Babylon. The other biblical prophets either lived after the exile, up to the fifth century BC, or they are hard to date.

Thus most of the prophets lived at times of national threat or disaster, and they proclaimed what they believed to be the 'words of God' to the nation in their desperate situation. They attempted to discern the purpose of their God in a history which is replete with tragedy and failure. After the monarchy of David and Solomon, in reality a rather insignificant kingdom, but later idealized as a golden age, the kingdom split into the two even more petty kingdoms of Israel and Judah. Those kingdoms were constantly threatened and eventually overcome by successive waves of imperial powers, including Egypt, Assyria, Babylon and Persia. In that situation, there were repeated revolutionary and prophetic movements calling for revolt against the imperialist overlords and the establishment of a renewed Israel, obedient to the Torah. The prophets took different views of what should be done, some arguing for alliances with the surrounding empires, and some urging a more isolationist policy. But gradually a set of common images was formed, based on a distinction between the old and the new age. The 'old age' was one of oppression by military empires. That age was coming to an end. The 'new age' was one where God would be rightly worshipped, and all nations would come to worship in the Temple in Jerusalem. The prophets used cosmic imagery of the fall of the stars from heaven (symbolizing the fall of the political powers of the world), a day of destruction and judgement on the nations, and a coming Saviour King, to convey these beliefs, thus associating political events with the realization of God's ultimate purpose for creation (with earth, and Jerusalem in particular, as its centre).

In reading the prophetic writings, it is important to take note of this imagery, and to note that when they seem to speak of the end of the world, a catastrophic judgement on the earth, and a new heaven and earth, they are commenting on political and historical events in terms of cosmic imagery which sees these things as anticipations of God's final purpose. What they say cannot be taken literally, for it is stated in poetic terms, using hyperbole, exaggeration and paradox as part of their rhetorical style. To take the prophetic oracles as literal predictions about the near future would render them false, since the world did not come to a sudden end. More importantly, it would be to miss the point, which is to evoke a discernment of the ultimate purpose of God as anticipated in the events of history, to evoke a perception of eternity in the events of time.

The prophet Zephaniah, for example, writing in the seventh century BC, when the kingdom of Judah was threatened by the Assyrians and the Babylonians, says: 'I will utterly sweep away everything from the face of the earth, says the LORD' (Zeph. 1.2). Even the birds and fish will be destroyed. 'The great day of the LORD is near' (1.14), a day of clouds and thick darkness. 'A full, a terrible end he will make of all the inhabitants of the earth' (1.18).

That seems definitive. Yet he goes on to say, 'Seek righteousness, seek humility; perhaps you may be hidden on the day of the LORD's wrath' (2.3). 'The LORD their God will be mindful of them and restore their fortunes' (2.7). A remnant will survive.

More than that, 'At that time I will change the speech of the peoples to a pure speech, that all of them may call on the name of the LORD' (3.9). Of Israel he says, 'I will make you renowned and praised among all the peoples of the earth' (3.20) – so there will be peoples of the earth left after all, who will turn to the Lord and serve him and honour the people of Israel.

The destruction of evil is spoken of in hugely exaggerated terms, as the destruction of all life on earth. This is then qualified by saying that a remnant of Israel will survive. It is further qualified by saying that many peoples will repent and serve the God of Israel.

It is very clear that such prophetic speeches cannot be taken literally. Perhaps there will be judgement, and there will be redemption. But these things are depicted in very rhetorical terms, with a lot of poetic licence. We might say that Zephaniah's prophecy was fulfilled, in that the Assyrian Empire fell and King Josiah initiated a programme of reforms. But any triumph of that sort was short-lived, since it was not long before the Babylonians overran Judah and took the people into captivity. It was certainly not an end of imperialism and a triumph for Israel.

The prophet Zephaniah spoke of an imminent extermination of the nations, the saving of a remnant of Israel, and a renewed world. Most of the other prophets whose words are recorded in the Bible said very similar things, though some are more pessimistic, some more optimistic, about the future. What they say is remarkably like what was said by some early Christians – a judgement on the nations, the creation of a 'remnant people', and a new age under the rule of Christ. In both cases, none of this happened, literally. It is not surprising that, on one view, Jesus joins a long line of Jewish prophets whose dreams of judgement, vindication and renewal were crushed on the wheel of history. On the other hand, soon after Jesus' death there was a catastrophic destruction of Israel and Jerusalem. There was the creation of a new covenant community, the Church. And there was the spread of that Church throughout the whole world. These were world-changing events, bringing in a new age in religious history.

Perhaps Jesus, like the prophets, was providing an interpretation of imminent events as historical anticipations of God's final goal for creation. In the end, all evil will be destroyed; the saints and martyrs who have given their lives in the long struggle against evil will be vindicated; and there will be a society of persons joyfully united to God for ever in love. These, however, need not be specific events within history. They may belong to an existence beyond history, when human history has come to an end, when God will be more clearly and intensely known by all. Within history, God acts continuously and in co-operation with human wills to call some to a special vocation to witness to God's purpose, and to create communities of love in a world filled with hatred.

Some events in history, however, are crucially disclosive of God's action and purpose. Within the biblical tradition, these would include the calling of Abraham, the exodus from Egypt, the building of the Temple in Jerusalem, and – for Christians – the life, death and resurrection of Jesus. They disclose the inner nature of spiritual reality in relation to the whole of human history, partially and ambiguously yet truly expressed in particular segments of history. And in doing so, they also disclose God's final goal for human history. They disclose the eternal in time.

It is these events that prophetic insight can discern. Such discernments are expressed in the poetic language of metaphor, a symbolic narrative that describes truths about the spiritual reality underlying the natural world of appearances in terms drawn from that natural world, but stretched beyond their normal uses.

Metaphorical narratives speak of a spiritual reality, a reality of consciousness, knowledge and bliss that underlies and gives rise to the whole of sensory reality. The images and symbols of such narratives evoke a view of this historical world as the expression, somehow flawed yet still authentic, of a deeper transcendent spiritual reality. They provide what could be called a religious explanation of the world, affirming that human life has a meaning, an enduring value and a purpose. To make such an affirmation is to explain, in a non-scientific sense, that the meaning of human life lies in its deep and essential relationship to a wider spiritual reality of which it is part.

Religious beliefs in the ancient world

We can see this use of metaphorical language in many of the religions of the ancient world. No doubt such metaphors were taken in many different ways. Some of these ways would be literal, though I think such literalizations are crude later falsifications, often by writers who no longer took them as serious religious symbols, of what were originally more clearly metaphorical in form.

For example, in the Greek symbol of Aurora, goddess of the dawn, it is 'as if' a beautiful goddess drew the dawn from the sea. But the goddess Aurora does not explain why the sun rises, and I find it odd for anyone with the slightest poetic sense to think that there was literally a goddess causing the dawn. The thought is rather that the beauty of the dawn discloses a transcendent reality, the hidden source of beauty and wonder. That reality is expressed by the symbol of Aurora. The use of the symbol does say that the dawn is not just a freak accident that arose by chance. The dawn discloses, for those who have eyes to see it, an underlying reality that is the source of all beauty, that envisages and creates beauty, and that delights in beauty. There is no beautiful but invisible woman there in the sky. But the image of a goddess may enable us to relate to natural phenomena as signs of personal (conscious, creative) presence. The image evokes and expresses a sense of quasi-personal relationship, a communication of spirit expressed in and through natural appearances.

It would demean this experience to think that it was a belief that there was a giant invisible woman hauling the sun from the sea. What the symbol is meant to do is to evoke a sense that there is a spiritual, conscious presence expressed in physical phenomena. The phenomena carry a reference beyond themselves to that which is their inner reality and source, a reality that the senses cannot reach. Many gods and goddesses of classical mythology represent the many aspects of how that presence is expressed, and are attempts to depict what the underlying nature of spirit is. It is not that positing a goddess, Aurora, explains why the sun rises each day. Quite the contrary, the rising of the sun becomes a symbol and manifestation of the beauty and fidelity of reality, whose inner nature is mind and spirit.

Seeing the world as full of gods, as the ancient Greeks did, is seeing the world we experience as filled with a transcendent presence, manifested in the beauty and terror of nature, before which the proper response is one of awe, reverence and fear. That presence is manifested in other ways too. There is a sense of moral objectivity, of obligation to respect and help others, of the proper way to live a fully human life, which seems to come to us as an existent ideal or demand to which we must respond. There is a sense of courage and patience that enables us to face hardship with resolution, and which presents the possibility of hope in times of death and destruction. There is a sense of creative inspiration and strength that can empower the imagination. There is a sense of vocation, of destiny and calling, that encourages us to use our unique gifts and talents. There is a reverence for ancestors that inspires us to hold firm to good traditions and to realize the aspirations our forbears had for us.

All these human experiences present themselves to many people as responses to something objective and estimable, known through ordinary everyday experiences, but also sometimes apprehended more intensely in crucial situations of human lives. The pantheon of gods depicts this reality in its various aspects, in symbols and images that enable devotees to respond to their experiences in what they feel to be more discerning and fulfilling ways.

Of course, I am interpreting the Greek metaphorical images of the gods as subtle and spiritually disclosive symbolic forms. Not all Greek myths are concerned with the spiritual life, and not all spiritual metaphors are of profound spiritual value. I am, however, suggesting that sets of spiritual metaphors for the pagan gods did have, at their best, a serious spiritual meaning, which was to evoke and sustain a sense of transcendence apprehended in many facets of experienced reality. The beginnings of Hebrew religion are not far removed from that.

Prophetic monotheism

There is nevertheless something quite distinctive about the biblical view of spiritual reality. In the Bible the Hebrew prophets gradually formulated the revolutionary belief that, unlike the Greek or Mesopotamian gods, there is just one spiritual reality underlying the natural world. There is only one God, who has a moral goal in creating the universe, an ideal to which the whole world moves. Human history is the arena in which this purpose is worked out, largely through struggle to overcome or redeem the misuses of freedom and desire which originate from the creation of societies of free human agents. The prophets express their perception of this moral goal by seeing key events of their history as anticipations of the goal. They saw God as active in helping humans to realize it or frustrating their self-centred and deluded efforts to oppose it, and as affirming the promise of its final attainment. So the key themes of prophecy are the warning of judgement on self-centred desire ('sin'), the call to struggle against evil with the help of God, and the promise of final liberation from evil.

In the course of their history, the prophets developed these themes with the aid of such metaphorical symbols as the fall of the sun and stars from the sky (the overthrow of the powers of historical oppression), the coming of a Son of Man on the clouds of heaven (the founding of a true Israel, or true human community, enveloped by the *Shekinah*, the cloud of the presence of the glory of God), the gathering of the elect from the four corners of the earth (the call of all peoples to accept God's gift of the Spirit of love), the Judgement Day (the fact that all would have to face the consequences of their moral choices), and the kingdom of God (the final reign of God in a world without evil).

Some people read the Bible as the actual history of the Israelites, just as it happened. But there is one extra character – God – who is an invisible person rewarding obedience with lots of sheep and fertility, and punishing disobedience by sending the Assyrians, Babylonians and Persians to overrun Israel and Judah. You can read the Bible that way, but there is something wrong with such a reading.

What is basically wrong is the very anthropomorphic idea of God that it involves, and the idea that the Bible provides just one continuous literal description of what happened in the history of Israel. These ideas are connected, because God appears in the one literal narrative as a more or less literally described person who arranges the affairs of history according to a rather neat and moralistic plan.

Jewish interpretations of the Bible are not as clear-cut as this. The Bible records events of history, true enough. But it records them from very different and often conflicting points of view. Sometimes it suggests that the good are always rewarded and the wicked are punished. But it often opposes such a moralistic view of history, with a recognition that rain falls on the just and unjust alike, that the innocent suffer, and that the hoped-for rule of peace and justice never completely arrives and never lasts very long. The history of Israel is a constantly renewed tragedy, and in Isaiah 40—55 ('second Isaiah'), for many the high point of prophetic writing, the best that can be hoped for is that future good will come out of the present suffering of Israel.

Since the advent of critical scholarship in the eighteenth century, most biblical scholars have seen the historical records as symbols of the transcendent reality of God, derived from a recon-structed past. Even before the rise of critical scholarship, medieval scholars like Aquinas saw that God is not an invisible person beyond the clouds, but the one changeless and timeless source of Being that appears to humans in various ways in accordance, not with real changes in God, but with changes in human attitudes and viewpoints.

Patristic and medieval theologians did not see God as a person who was sometimes pleased and sometimes angry. They saw God as absolute Beauty and Perfection, changeless in being, discerned in different ways because of the inadequacy of all human concepts to capture such a reality.

The interpretation of biblical statements about God will largely depend on your view of what sort of being God is. If God is the changeless source of all Being, all talk of God speaking with or to the prophets will be metaphorical. For instance, when God has a conversation with Abraham in which they seem to bargain about how many inhabitants of Sodom would be needed to save it from destruction (Gen. 18.23–33), no medieval theologian would have thought that God was actually prepared to change his mind. This was, after all, an account of a conversation between a wholly changeless God and a human being. Even if you depict God as entering into relationship with finite agents, that relationship will be of a quite unique kind. It will be an accommodation of the infinite reality of God to what human minds can understand. Those minds may well have a very limited understanding, and prophets may even misinterpret some of the apprehensions of God they have in visions, dreams and oracular possessions. Such misapprehensions are recorded quite often in the Bible. One instance is Jeremiah 14.13–14, where many prophets are said by Jeremiah to be deceived, even though no doubt they were doing their best. The major biblical prophets are usually thought to be at least on the right lines, which is why they got into the Bible. There is no indication, however, that what they say is truly and absolutely what God has directly said to them.

Once we see the prophetic histories as human writings inspired by claimed apprehensions of the transcendent God, we can readily recognize the diversity of human perspectives they convey, and the historical context in which they stand. We can then more readily distinguish between the great themes of biblical prophecy and the details contained in specific oracles or historical narratives. Those great themes are what is most distinctive and authentic in the very varied and argumentative tradition of Hebrew prophecy.

They include the theme of covenant or vocation, the sense that Israel is set apart by God to worship God truly as the supreme moral Ideal.

There is the theme of moral and ritual law, laying down demands of justice and of a total commitment of life to God, the supreme good and the source and goal of all creation (a commitment that is symbolized and expressed in the Temple sacrificial rituals).

There is the theme of prophecy, claiming that God demands justice, punishes selfishness and injustice, and promises renewal.

There is the theme of kingship, developed after the institution of the kings of Israel and Judah, which develops into the idea of a Messiah, or God-appointed leader of Israel.

There is the theme of exodus, or liberation from slavery into a new life of freedom and a community of justice and peace.

And there is the theme of Apocalypse (visionary 'revelations' of the end of time), developing during and after the return from exile in Babylon, with its dreams of a dawning kingdom that will establish God's total rule and sovereignty.

All these themes develop gradually, accumulating new layers of meaning in new historical circumstances. If we continue the trajectory of their development, we can perhaps see that there is a growing recognition that the goal of history lies beyond history, in sharing the life of God. It is not a physical life in a future earthly Jerusalem, but a radically new creation in which all people, living and dead, can share.

God's purpose is human fulfilment in a compassionate and co-operative community. That is the ideal to which the law points.

Evil destroys the self, but that self can be renewed by the Spirit of God – that is the reality to which talk of divine judgement and mercy points.

All humans are called to self-sacrificial service of perfect goodness, and to the pursuit of restorative justice – that is the fulfilment of the sacrifices of the Temple.

Above all, our ultimate loyalty is to love the Good, a good embedded in a supreme consciousness which is aware of human suffering and which liberates us for a higher life in God. Moreover, that supreme consciousness is not just a remote and impersonal Ideal, but relates to human lives as a compassionate, loving, and suffering Saviour God.

There are the spiritual ideals to which the history of Israel points, insofar as it moves beyond narrow nationalism and vindictive seeking for retribution upon the wicked, towards a universal care for all peoples and a hope for the redemption of the whole world.

These ideals can and do exist within Judaism, for the people of the covenant continue to exist in a special relation to the God who appeared to Abraham. Fortunately for those of us who are Gentiles, it also exists, by divine grace, in the Christian faith, which has taken a form of Messianic Judaism into the Gentile world, and speaks of a new covenant and a new Israel, not replacing the old, but standing in solidarity with it as a radically new form of prophetic and Messianic faith.

Are there immoral rules in the Old Testament?

—◆—

This may all sound very fine. But for some people the negative aspects of the Bible – its occasional descent into chauvinism, its sometimes vindictive attitudes towards the 'enemies of God's people', and its sometimes harsh penal laws – outweigh its very real positive aspects. We bring our own feelings, values and beliefs to a reading of the Bible. If we dislike the idea of some supreme authority telling us what to do, if we regard religion as repressive, rule-bound and joyless, and if we value human freedom above all, we are likely to read the Bible as a sad history of human errors. Richard Dawkins regards the biblical God as 'arguably the most unpleasant character in all fiction: jealous and proud of it; a petty, unjust, unforgiving control-freak; a vindictive, bloodthirsty ethnic cleanser, a misogynistic, homophobic, racist, infanticidal, genocidal, filicidal, pestilential, megalomaniacal, sadomasochistic, capriciously malevolent bully' (*The God Delusion*, Bantam, London, 2006, p. 31).

What this shows is that our reading of a text is greatly influenced by our own prior beliefs. Dawkins is reading the same text as those who think that God is universally loving, wise, perfectly just, merciful and all-forgiving, desirous of the fulfilment of all human and non-human creation. How can there be such different readings of the same text? The fundamental reason is that the text contains many different human responses to what is apprehended of God at very different times in Hebrew history. What Dawkins does, and what many religious believers have also done, is to take all these responses as truly describing God just as they stand. They ignore completely the possibility that there is moral change and development in the Bible, as there is in general human history.

To take just one example, Dawkins describes God as 'homophobic'. Homophobia is fear or hatred of homosexuals. It is a radically new moral perception in some societies that homosexuality is morally acceptable, and it is far from being universally accepted even now. 'Homophobia' is a rather new vice, and for most cultures throughout human history homosexuality has been regarded as morally unacceptable. Biblical laws on this subject are pretty ancient, and entirely typical of their culture. Homosexuality is biblically regarded as an 'abomination', just as adultery is. Nevertheless, any Jewish commentator would point out that hatred of homosexuals is a vice, and is quite different from prohibition of homosexual practice. So it is inaccurate to accuse God of hating those who perform immoral and prohibited acts. God still cares for their ultimate good (it may be worth pointing out that eternal hell-fire is not an Old Testament idea).

In a similar way, it is inaccurate to accuse God of hating women or of hating Gentiles (being misogynistic or racist), even if it were true that God's law subordinates women to men in some respects, or forbids Jews to marry Gentiles. We can see here how disagreement with certain widely held moral rules can lead someone to confuse disapproval of a practice with hatred of persons, and see the views they disagree with as malevolent or despicable. Strong emotions are engaged, and ways of life other than one's own are seen as evil or sub-human. This is a very good example of the sort of thing Dawkins criticizes in religious people – they sometimes confuse rejection of certain human practices with hatred and intolerance of those who practise them, however conscientiously. Well, at least, we might say, this fault is not confined to the religious.

Still, the question remains: are some ancient biblical rules not ones that we should now, in our enlightened times, reject or amend? I think the answer is yes, we should. And many have been amended. Jewish Rabbis (lawyers) have amended almost all the rules laying down penalties like stoning to death. They have various reasons for doing so, one of which is that they are in tension with other laws like 'loving your neighbour as yourself'. Law is not easy, which is why there are so many lawyers. And even the laws of God have to be applied in new situations, and consistently with other laws that may suggest modifications to them. Laws believed to be literally God-given were given in a specific social context and at a specific time (many of them as far back as the Bronze Age). It would be ludicrous to try to apply them literally in very different contexts, and so lawyers need to work out the underlying principles behind such laws, and see how they can best be applied. It may turn out that distinctions can be made between promiscuous and perverse sexual practices, and ways of expressing genuine love and fidelity between partners of the same sex, and the biblical laws could be clarified and applied accordingly.

There are virtually no Orthodox Jewish Rabbis who would apply all the biblical laws just as they stand. They are commented on at length in the Talmud, which contains many diverse interpretations of the laws. Laws concerning stoning to death, for example, are never applied because there is no supreme council or Sanhedrin to apply them. Moreover, mercy and restraint were always held to override the strict application of the law. So even those who think that God dictated these laws to Moses believe that God continues to inspire the reflections and decisions of Rabbis to re-interpret the laws in new situations. No law can be considered on its own, but only as part of a complex and developing tradition of juridical practice, requiring great knowledge and practical wisdom.

Some Christians misunderstand this, and read the laws of the Pentateuch without any reference to judicial practice and community consensus. They then take the laws in a strict and inflexible sense, that would not occur to any instructed Jew. In that way, Christians can be much more literalist and fundamentalist than Jews. But that is a result of simply failing to see what biblical law, the Torah, really is.

For many Jews, and for almost all Christians, there is a more radical alternative. That is to say that we are not bound by the 613 biblical statutes and ordinances of the Torah. Christians decisively renounced the Torah at the first Council of the Church in Jerusalem (Acts 15), and regard most of its laws as no longer binding. So they are committed to saying that God can rescind or radically revise revealed laws. Liberal Jews and Christians suggest that God did not literally dictate the laws to Moses anyway. The laws were built up over generations, edited into various collections, and ascribed to Moses much later.

This view is quite consistent with believing that God inspired the process of law-making, giving a succession of prophetic lawyers a deepened insight into what justice and mercy require, and a practical wisdom into what is necessary for a healthy and integrated society of originally nomadic tribes in a largely hostile environment, surrounded by potential enemies. Most importantly, the idea of God connected the law and morality of the Hebrews with the idea of a categorically binding moral authority and with a God who could be loved and enjoyed as well as being obeyed as an objective source of supreme goodness.

Those opposed to religion would see this as giving imaginary supernatural sanctions to man-made rules, thus making human authority beyond criticism and supremely repressive. But it may alternatively be interpreted as seeing that justice and mercy are rooted in objective reality, and are thus supremely important in themselves. Such an objective grounding for the law separates it from the political decisions of tyrants, and provides a basis for moral criticism of rulers.

It does not follow that we know with certainty what the objective moral truth is (what God, if perceived adequately, really requires). All we know is what we *think* is just ('what God requires' being the same thing), from our own limited cultural and historical viewpoint. What is important is that there is a moral truth to be found. It may be equally important to stress that we may not yet have found it in its fullness.

It may be a fairly common religious mistake to think that we know the mind of God. But if what we have are the responses of limited human minds to the perceived presence and purposes of God then, even if those human minds are inspired to greater than usual insight by God, their knowledge may be far from infallible.

What the Bible seems to show is a gradual development of spiritual and moral beliefs which roughly reflects changes in such beliefs in cultural history. In morality, the most obvious example is the command to exterminate the inhabitants of Canaan (Deut. 20.16). I cannot believe that a God of mercy and love would command such a thing. But I can believe that people might be so devoted to one God that they think any other form of worship must be exterminated. Their belief would be false, and it arises from a perverted idea of what loyalty to God requires.

This is a command which should not be obeyed. It almost certainly never was obeyed. And it is overridden by the command to 'love foreigners' which is found in Leviticus 19.34. But we have to admit that a command is attributed to God which is abhorrent, and expresses an unreconstructed hatred for other religions and cultures.

It follows that the Bible contains false statements about morality which all morally right-minded people should renounce. But the Bible contains innumerable statements that override Deuteronomy 20. The later prophets, in particular, repeatedly enjoin mercy on enemies. And for Christians, Jesus' statement, 'love your neighbour', which Luke explicitly applies to a Samaritan, a person of a different religious belief, is decisive.

Some rules in the Bible are immoral. But that does not mean, as Dawkins says, that God is 'a bloodthirsty ethnic cleanser'. It means that some early Hebrews were (or at least thought that their forebears should have been). They misunderstood completely what God was like, and mistakenly put into God's mouth their own perverse sentiments. So is God a projection of human moral beliefs? No, not quite. We can see the developing moral history of the Hebrews as a continual struggle to formulate a set of principles for human flourishing in relation to a transcendent God. Their moral rules were not only about the relation of persons to one another, as in a wholly secular morality. They were also about the relation of persons, and especially of a particular society, the 'covenant people', to God, the spiritual source of reality.

The prophets apprehended God, in dreams, visions, extraordinary providential or miraculous events, and inner experience. But they apprehended God in ways limited by their personalities and social practices. Sometimes their interpretations of such apprehensions were malign – as in thinking that loyalty to God meant the destruction of opposing beliefs. Sometimes they were sublime – as when Jesus taught that God's universal love entailed love even of enemies. There is no inerrancy. There is diversity. And there is development, from more vengeful to more compassionate views.

If this is so, the question for a reader of the Bible should not be 'What did God say?' but 'How did these people see God? What did they think God's purpose was? How adequate was their view?' The Bible will then not be a reference book of moral commands, which we must simply obey without question. It will be a record of developing (and sometimes decaying) insights into the nature and purpose of God, from which we can learn, but which we must test against the highest biblical standard we can find.

That standard is not hidden away obscurely. For Christians, it is the standard of Jesus' life and teaching, which is the fulfilment of all previous alleged apprehensions of God and the paradigm against which they must be judged. By that standard Deuteronomy 20.16 is seen to be so inadequate as to be actually perverse. But I do not suppose there is any Christian who would take that text as a beginning point for Christian moral teaching. We need to explain why it is there in the Bible. And the most reasonable answer is that it is there as part of the record of what people have thought about God, and how they have sometimes got it almost completely wrong, even when they were no doubt sincerely worshipping the true God. It is a warning to us to beware of falling into intolerance in the name of God, and a warning that it is all too easy to do so. But we have a higher standard in Jesus Christ.

So we can take the dangerous text as a positive reminder to root out in our own lives all that might lead us away from true discipleship, however tempting it might be. Admittedly with a slight sense of strain, we can give even this text a positive spiritual interpretation (and a frankly metaphorical one), asking what it says to us about total commitment to God – perhaps that it requires putting to death all desires that hold us back from God. But if we keep Christ at the forefront of our minds, we will not be tempted to take it as a licence to kill or oppress those who disagree with us.

Part 3

BIBLICAL METAPHORS AND CHRISTIAN DOCTRINES

Metaphor in the Bible

As I have suggested, to understand the Bible properly, we need to be aware of both diversity and development in the biblical writings. We need a good sense of history, to see the contexts in which the various texts were written, and the sorts of knowledge and understanding that were available to the writers. We also need to be sensitive to the importance of metaphorical language throughout the Bible. *Metaphors are statements that are literally false, or false in their primary sense,* but that communicate truth in an indirect and sometimes cryptic form. Not all the Bible is metaphorical, of course. Jesus really did die on the cross and rise from death – that is no metaphor. Yet the meaning of Jesus' death and resurrection is conveyed by metaphors – Jesus is the 'lamb of God' and he 'sits at the right hand of God'. But Jesus is not literally a young sheep who sits in an armchair. Usually we only get at the spiritual meaning of the Bible when we see the importance of metaphors, and what sort of truth they can convey.

There is certainly much use of metaphor in the Bible. When Jesus says, 'If your right eye causes you to sin, tear it out' (Matt. 5.29), few suppose that he meant us to do this literally. Readers may dispute about just what this sentence means, but it is certainly metaphorical – that is, what it appears to suggest is literally false (we should not actually tear our eyes out), but it suggests, in a cryptic and challenging way, some sort of truth (perhaps that we should not let sexual desire dominate our lives).

One main point of metaphor is that though what it says could be stated literally in a straightforward way, it would not have such richness. It rather invites the imagination to think of various possibilities, and look for a meaning which speaks to us in our condition – and that condition will vary from one person to another. It is important to metaphor that different interpretations should appeal to different people, and that none of those interpretations will be finally and uniquely correct. Some interpretations will be sillier than others – a literal interpretation would be very silly. But there is a range of sensible interpretations, each of which may speak to someone in a special way, but some of which may not speak to everyone. *A metaphor suggests many possible connotations, which readers have to think out for themselves. There is not one literal and correct meaning.*

When metaphors are used in a spiritual text, they carry a primarily spiritual meaning. They refer not to ordinary everyday things and events, but to how we are to think of and respond to the supreme spiritual reality of God. The eye, in Jesus' metaphor, is not just the physical bodily eye. It is the organ of spiritual perception, that by means of which we might apprehend God in and through all things. When 'the eye causes you to sin', that is not some odd sort of ocular event. It is a misuse of the sense of spiritual apprehension. It occurs when we attend to and concentrate on things that separate us from the vision of God – such as sexual activity that uses other persons solely as objects of pleasure, for example.

It is this corruption of vision that needs to be rooted out. Tearing out physical eyes would not help – we could carry on fantasizing about degrading sex in our minds. We need to re-orient our way of apprehending things, so that we see other persons (including attractive men and women) as images of God and temples of the Spirit, and not solely as stimulants to our own egoistic desires. So the metaphor directs us to spiritual vision or seeing, and warns us against cultivating desires and propensities that will lead us away from seeing God in all things.

Spiritual metaphors seem to be talking about physical things and events. But taken in that way they are literally false. They are really talking about spiritual realities – that is, realities that are non-physical, but that have some form of consciousness and agency. They are talking especially about the reality of God, and how we are to think of or relate to God, the supreme spiritual reality. *Spiritual metaphors refer primarily to God, who is infinitely far beyond any literal description.* They suggest how we might think of or react to God – though always in an inadequate way.

There are many such metaphors in the Bible. God is spoken of in the book of Revelation as seated on a throne, with a lamb with seven horns and seven eyes standing nearby among 24 elders dressed in white, with golden crowns on their heads.

The text makes it clear that this is a vision rather than a literal seeing. But even as a vision, what is 'seen' are symbols (visual metaphors), not literal objects. The lamb is Jesus, who is not a physical lamb with many horns and eyes. The visionary appearance represents something else – and the text in this case actually tells us that the horns and eyes represent seven spirits. The 'slain lamb' represents the crucified Jesus, slaughtered to redeem God's people. The glorious shining figure on the throne represents the glory and power and beauty of God. But if anyone thinks that God is actually a physical human form on a physical throne, however glorious, they have made a terrible mistake.

The Bible declares that there can be no physical image of God, whether earthly or heavenly ('You shall not make for yourself an idol, whether in the form of anything that is in heaven above, or that is on the earth beneath'; Exod. 20.4), and that God is radically unlike anything we can imagine ('To whom then will you liken God, or what likeness compare with him?' Isa. 40.18). So at once we know two things about these symbols. First, they do not literally depict God. Second, as symbols they refrain from telling us exactly what God is, but they direct the mind and imagination to search for an underlying spiritual reality. There will be many different particular interpretations, but we can hardly fail to see that they represent God as powerful and beautiful, in a way that is far beyond any visual representation.

'God sits on a throne' (cf. Ezek. 1.26) is a metaphor, and it asks us to think of kings, who do sit on thrones, and to think of ways in which the good properties of kingship might apply to God, but in a way that we cannot literally depict, since God is infinitely greater than any king. For many people the image of kingship might be unhelpful, since it conjures up thoughts of tyranny or paternalism. Yet with a little imagination we can think of a totally wise and compassionate ruler, fully responsive to all the wishes of his people. Then we can see what the biblical image suggests, even though in a very different culture we might want to use a different image, such as that of a trusted, and perhaps feminine, companion and guide. The Old Testament provides such an image in its symbol of Lady Wisdom, who 'was set up at the first, before the beginning of the earth' (Prov. 8.23). This image was later used by Christians to denote both Christ and the Holy Spirit, and it is a useful complement to the image of God as King.

In a similar way, when we say that Jesus 'sits at the right hand of God', we are directed to think of those who are especially close to kings and mediate their powers to others, and to see that Jesus is infinitely more than that, yet that Jesus is associated with God in a uniquely intimate way.

There is no *doctrine* here, no exact specification of just what the relation of Jesus to God is, in an accurate philosophical way. There is just the metaphor, which is intentionally cryptic and diffuse, calling us to think beyond its literal meaning to a whole set of possible figurative meanings, all of which we must transcend if we are to understand the nature of Jesus as 'Son of God' (another metaphor, of course, since Jesus is not a male product of God's genes). It would be positively misleading to take 'Jesus sits at the right hand of God' literally, as that would give the impression that Jesus and God were two quite different people – and if anything is wrong about the Trinity, that is, since 'The Lord our God, the Lord, is one' (Mark 12.29).

Metaphors of creation

———◆———

The relation between the metaphorical language of the Bible and the more austere philosophical language of later Christian doctrines is complex. There is no doubt that there are doctrines in the Bible. God created the universe; God reveals the divine nature and purpose through the prophets and, for Christians, supremely through Jesus; God acts to liberate humans from evil; and God's Spirit unites humanity to God.

But these doctrines are not systematically expounded, and they are clothed with all the mystery and many-sidedness of metaphor. Thus any attempt to construct a theology, a systematic exposition of Christian belief using the best available knowledge of the day, will employ and interpret the metaphors in different ways. What I would like to do is to evoke a sense of the inadequacy of the human mind to frame any finally adequate theology, and accordingly to encourage Christians to be rather tentative about their own interpretations, and rather appreciative of the differing interpretations of others.

In this spirit, I will examine some chief biblical metaphors that are relevant to the doctrines of creation, incarnation, atonement and salvation. Without claiming to give any sort of final interpretation, I will suggest how those metaphors might be interpreted in the light of our modern post-Enlightenment culture of science-inspired critical enquiry. My main conclusion will be that ancient doctrines may well need to be re-formulated, and the more literalist interpretations may prove very hard or even impossible to defend, but that the core spiritual meanings of the biblical metaphors remain important and illuminating.

Christian theologians have usually seen that almost all biblical descriptions of God are metaphors. One of the most important sets of metaphorical descriptions of God and the activity of God are found in the biblical stories of creation (Gen. 1.1—2.4 and

Gen. 2.5–25). Theologians like Augustine believed that the stories of creation in Genesis were extended metaphors for the way in which we should think of God as creator of the universe.

How, after all, could a nomadic group of tribespeople in a Middle Eastern desert, who knew nothing of the real nature of stars and planets, or of the size and age of the universe, think about God's creation? God does not in Scripture reveal scientific truths that might have come in useful a few thousand years later, like the Theory of Relativity or the value of Planck's Constant. That is not the sort of thing the Bible does, and if it had done, it would have been totally incomprehensible to its hearers. The message of Genesis is a spiritual message, a message about how we should think of God – though we must always be careful to add that God will always be infinitely greater than we think. So the appropriate language to use will be the language of metaphor.

If that message is to be put in a metaphorical way, then the metaphors will not be literally true, but they will convey spiritual truths in a cryptic and imaginative way that can produce deep personal insights about our own relation to God. So that is what the Genesis creation accounts are most likely to be. It is what Augustine and most early Christian theologians thought they were. They present a set of metaphors for conveying what it is literally impossible to state clearly, how we must think of God in relation to our own lives and to the whole known universe.

The most important truth the first Genesis creation story conveys is that God is the one and only creator of everything that exists. The metaphors the Bible uses are taken from accounts that may have been familiar to the early Hebrew tribes. They are taken from the ancient Babylonian and Sumerian creation stories. But they adapt these stories in a new way. In the Babylonian story many gods arise from chaos and fight each other. In the Bible there is only one God who creates all things. That is an important and new spiritual truth.

Nevertheless, metaphors quickly enter into the account. God says, 'Let there be light'; God sees it and thinks it good. Yet God does not literally speak – with what vocal chords, since God has no body and no throat? God does not literally see, since God has no eyes, and does not even need eyes. You might easily miss the fact that these are metaphors, since we have got so used to them. But they are metaphors – the text says that God speaks and sees, but that cannot be literally true, since God has no body.

What is the spiritual meaning of speaking and seeing? I have emphasized that the whole point of metaphors is that you cannot give one correct literal interpretation. But you can say what they suggest to you about the nature of God and how we must think of God. So we might say that 'God speaking' points to something in God like the occurrence of a thought, and 'God seeing' points to something in God like knowledge. This suggests that the universe does not come about by chance, but that it is the result of knowledge and thought, the result of something like a conscious decision or intention.

Immediately the great theologians of Christianity – people like Augustine, who wrote a commentary on the creation story – would warn us that we must not think we have understood God precisely when we say that God thinks and knows. God's thoughts are not our thoughts, or anything like our thoughts. God, says Augustine, as the creator of space and time, is beyond space and time, and so is not in either space or time. So God does not think one thing after another – that would take time. God does not first of all (on the first day) decide to create light, and later on (on the second day) decide to create the sky. God's thoughts are timeless, and do not come one after another.

So Augustine says that talk of the six 'days' of creation must be metaphorical. It cannot be talking about six separate things that God does, one after another. Indeed, for Augustine, because God is not in time at all, the whole of space and time must be created by God in one timeless act.

So what does the story mean by speaking of 'days'? Well, this is a metaphor, so we must look for a spiritual meaning. Augustine supposes that the 'days' represent, not temporal periods of time at all, but logical distinctions between sorts of created things. You do not have to believe Augustine – there is not just one correct inter-pretation of a metaphor like 'days'. But it could be that Genesis is saying that there are different orders of created things, different kinds of things that exist, and all of them are created solely by one supreme God, who has created them through something like – but also very unlike, in their human forms – knowledge and will.

Perhaps we may think that, even if God creates everything in one and the same timeless creative act, still from the point of view of people in time, God has brought things into existence one after another. First come photons (light), some of the most primitive elements from which the whole universe will be built. Second, from a human point of view, comes the formation of an atmosphere on this planet (the sky). Third, land-masses emerge and simple forms of biological life begin (plants). Fourth, the sun, moon and stars become visible as the clouds that cover the earth's surface begin to clear.

Incidentally, the stars are described in Hebrew literally as 'sanctuary lamps' in the sky, hanging from the dome of the sky, and below the 'waters beyond the dome'. This just emphasizes the point that these are not literal statements, even though (I am tentatively suggesting) the account does give an illuminating account of the gradual development of life on earth over a long period of time. We know that the stars are not lamps hung on a dome, but stars many millions of light-years away in space. But the ancient Hebrews would not have comprehended that, and anyway the purpose of the Bible is not to provide astronomical information, but to present a set of metaphors that will be spiritually meaningful. In this respect, it could be spiritually important to say that the stars are not gods (as they were in some cultures), but that they shine to the glory of God, and that the whole cosmos is God's temple. The spiritual meaning is both important and true, and since it is given in metaphors, like most statements about God in the Bible, it misses the point to ask if these statements are literally true in a physical sense.

Nevertheless, I think there could be a spiritual point in dividing the creation up into 'days', since it points to the fact that more complex forms of organic life are emergent from simpler forms. So humans, when they emerge rather late in earth's history, are not totally different in kind from other material things. In fact, they *are* material things ('made of dust', according to the second creation story), and it may be a very important fact that they spring from, and are an integral part of, the whole material world. They are not alien intruders, associated with matter for a short while and then destined to be free of it. Their destiny is bound up with the destiny of the physical universe, and God saw that creation was good long before any humans existed. That may be an important spiritual point, reminding us that the natural world has its own form of sacredness, that we are an intrinsic part of it, and that we should appreciate and care for it precisely because it is God's creation.

The first Genesis story ends with the last two days of creation. On the fifth day, fish, sea-monsters and birds are created. Since birds are generally thought to be descended from dinosaurs, this could easily be made to match the evolutionary process of life on earth, in which dinosaurs preceded the rise of the mammals. Since I have denied that the literal truth is what is important, I would not want to put too much stress on that interpretation. But I find it interesting, all the same.

On the sixth day, the animals (mammals?) are created, and among them human beings. According to the Bible, humans are not different from other animals in having an immortal soul. All animals are breathed into by God, and receive the breath of life (*neshemah*). Humans are no different from other animals in this respect (cf. Gen. 7.15).

Where humans differ, according to Genesis, is that they are made in the image and likeness of God (Gen. 1.26). That means, not that they look like God or that they are replicas of God in any way – again, a literal interpretation of the word for 'image', which is a 'physical idol or statue', can only be misleading – but that they are given responsibility for caring for God's created earth. As God acts to create and sustain and enjoy and love the earth, so should human beings. They are the only animals on this planet who have the knowledge and power to order living things peaceably, and bring out the full beauty of creation by cultivating the earth, and 'subduing it' where necessary. They must obviously do so responsibly, and in the knowledge that God is the ultimate owner of all created things. Humans cannot do whatever they like with the earth and its inhabitants. They must be careful to fulfil God's purposes.

Here once more Genesis is different from the Babylonian creation story, which makes humans the slaves of the gods. Humans, according to Genesis, are not slaves, but 'walk with God in the garden'. That is, they are created to be companions of God, and to do God's will in a creative and responsible way.

The spiritual lessons of Genesis are profound. They form the truth of what the accounts are saying in their metaphorical way. To try to take them literally would be to miss the spiritual meaning, and reduce the symbolism of Scripture to a pedestrian description of remote physical events. That is why, when Augustine wrote 'On the Literal Meaning of Genesis', he affirmed that the 'literal' (real) meaning of the text was symbolic. God's one creative act of making all things timelessly was portrayed as a gradual process taking six days. There was a reason for that, and I have suggested the sort of reason it might be, just as Augustine did. So if we want to understand Genesis properly, we have to see that it is a metaphorical narrative with a spiritual meaning. It is not a literal description of events that no human being could possibly have seen. A literal description of the beginning of the universe would have meant precisely nothing to the ancient Hebrews.

One vital thing to remember is that creation is not really about the beginning of the universe at all. It is about the relation of every time and place to a creator God who is beyond all time and space, and whose inner nature is indescribable in literal terms. Lots of people are misled into thinking that 'the creation' is the beginning of the universe. That is misleading if it leads anyone to think that God created the universe at the beginning, and then did nothing ever after.

Augustine rightly pointed out that God creates time itself, from beginning to end. So every moment is directly created by God – as Jesus said, 'My Father is still working, and I also am working' (John 5.17). Each moment of time is the direct creation of God. So it does not really matter how long the universe has existed, or even whether it has existed for ever, without temporal beginning. The universe is created by God, however much time there is in it, as long as every time and every space depends wholly upon the will of God for its existence.

What does Genesis mean, then, by speaking of God's 'rest' on the seventh day? It does not seem possible to take this literally. You cannot believe that God stopped doing any creative work when God set the universe up. How long, anyway, would the seventh day last? For the rest of time? Or does God need one day a week off creating, so that on Saturdays (the seventh day in Jewish thought), God is not creating anything, that God does a six-day week?

It is much easier if you do not have to take 'day' literally. You might then say that, just as there is a time to be creative, so there is a time for rest and enjoyment of what has been created. In the case of God, these things do not have to come one after another. God can 'work' and 'rest', create and enjoy, at the same time. But in the case of humans, who have to try to imitate God in a very feeble way, we do need to divide time up into periods of creative work and periods of appreciative rest.

So the 'Sabbath rest' is for our sake, not God's. We need to set aside one day in seven for appreciating God's creation and for contemplating the beauty of God. We are doing, in a 'spread-out' way, spread out over a week, what in God is beyond time altogether. In Jewish thought, the Sabbath rest is not just lying about doing nothing. It is seeking the deepest personal fulfilment by conscious relationship to God. It is not an energetic doing, a changing of the physical world. It is a contemplative resting in God, in which all the deepest capacities of mind and spirit are engaged.

Perhaps this points to the fact that God, as Supreme Goodness and Beauty, is an object of eternal delight, that God delights in the divine Being itself. This same God creates the universe in order that others should share in that delight, and in order that new finite forms of goodness and beauty should exist. Since the created universe is spread out in time, we can think of God as working and then as resting. But, as Jesus pointed out, God really never ceases both to work and to 'rest' (to contemplate perfect goodness and to create finite images of it in the universe).

A profound teaching of the six-day creation story is that what is in God one unbounded, infinite and timeless ocean of Being, is expressed in the universe in many bounded, finite and temporal forms. The universe progressively reveals the nature of God, and moves towards a state in which finite persons, fully parts of the material universe, can enter consciously into a relationship of love and union with God. The 'six days' all continue to co-exist, but are completed when they are taken up into that response to God which human beings can bring to full awareness.

The seventh day is not a period of time during which God does nothing. It is the fulfilment of all things in God, the final completion of all the orders of creation, when time is taken into eternity, and the whole temporal process of divine self-expression is returned in full consciousness to the one from whom it emanated. How much grander is this vision of the creative unfolding of God into an emergent creation, and the return of creation to its creator, than a literal description of what happened in one short week a few thousand years ago!

The decisive clue to the inner spiritual meaning of Genesis is Jesus' remark, 'My Father is still working'. God creates and God delights (rests) in creation, and we, God's creatures, can enter both into God's creative activity and into God's delight. We are integral parts of the material universe, but parts that have become capable of understanding and creative action, and thus of uniting the material creation to the Supreme Spirit from which it proceeds.

Metaphors of incarnation

For Christians, there is even more to the Genesis account than this. The word that God speaks in creation is the eternal Word who was enfleshed, embodied, incarnate, in Jesus. That word was not spoken once, long ago, and then faded away. It exists beyond time and for ever, and all particular words and forms are splintered fragments of its all-embracing unity. The Word of God, the *Logos* referred to in the first chapter of John's Gospel (John 1.1), is the thought, the reason, the intellect, mind or wisdom, of God.

This fact is a reminder that *biblical metaphors need to be interpreted in the light of the whole range of similar metaphors throughout the Bible.*

The fact that many different English words are needed to interpret one apparently simple phrase helps to show what is meant by the metaphorical nature of the 'Word'. Taken literally, it would be absurd to say that Jesus was the noun or adjective of God. It would also be misleading, since a 'word' is something impersonal and inactive. It is a communication from a person, but it is not itself a person in any sense. Jesus, however, is a person, and if we say that he embodies the Word of God, we do not mean that he is really a grammatical part of speech.

In unpacking the metaphor, we have to ask what words do, and there are many suggestions we might make. One is that words express the thoughts, the mind and intention, of their speaker. They communicate or externalize what is in the speaker's mind.

Now the eternal Word that was with God in the beginning cannot be the historical person of Jesus, who was born and began to be as a human person at a particular time in history. So the eternal expression of the mind of God is something much greater than the human Jesus. Most ancient theologians said that it is the pattern or archetype of all created things. Thus the letter to the Colossians says that 'He is the image of the invisible God . . . for in him all things in heaven and on earth were created . . . all things have been created through him . . . he himself is before all things, and in him all things hold together' (Col. 1.15–17).

The 'he' referred to here is no human person. Indeed, it is no finite object at all. It exists before all things, it contains all things, and all things are created through it. This Word, greater than the universe, containing the universe ('everything in heaven and earth'), is nothing other than the primordial expression of the divine mind. To call it 'the intelligible blueprint of all creation' would not be out of place.

Yet even this seems too limited a conception for the expression of a God who is beyond human comprehension. So the letter to the Colossians, and the New Testament as a whole, uses another metaphor, that of the 'Son of God'. Unlike 'Word', this is a personal metaphor. But if taken literally it too can mislead, if it leads us to think of God's wisdom as another person in addition to God. The fact is that the Son of God is not different from God. It is God, but God manifesting in a particular way.

The eternal Son is not different in being from the Father (he is, as the Nicene Creed puts it, 'of one substance with the Father'), so we have to ask why we should speak of a 'Son of God' at all. I suggest that in speaking of a 'Father' we are speaking of the ultimate source or cause of all things, that primordial and boundless reality from which all things originate and in which they have their being. Being boundless, it cannot be fully understood by any finite mind, and so there is a real sense in which it must always remain transcendent, apart, unknowable, as it is in its own inner reality.

However, God also relates positively to the universe as its creator (and perhaps towards many created universes, for all we know). In that respect, there is an aspect of God that is more intelligible or comprehensible to us, which forms the pattern of our created world, and which generates an image of the inner and infinite divine nature that we can more easily relate to. In expressing the nature of the Father in a particular personal form, and in truly expressing the Father's will and purpose for a created world, this aspect of the divine could be called the 'Son', the image and expression, of 'the Father', the transcendent cause of all things.

This intellectual exploration of the metaphor of 'Son' would relate it closely to the metaphor of 'Word', but would add a less impersonal and passive element. The image of a son connotes something living and active and capable of personal relationship. That adds something new to the image of a word, with which we could not properly speaking have a personal relationship. If we hold both metaphors together, we might think of the intelligible blueprint of creation not just as a sort of architect's drawing, but as a direct and immediate expression of the living, active and personal aspect of the divine being.

I do not think that I have just given the one correct account of divine Sonship, or of the two aspects of the Christian God that we call Father and Son. I am simply exploring the metaphors, trying to bring out my personal perspective (a rather abstract philosophical one, to be sure) on what they convey to me. It is essential to the nature of metaphors that we should not be led into theological mistakes by taking them literally (so that Father and Son are two different persons or beings), but equally we should not pretend that there is just one unpacking of their meaning that is correct. The best word for what they are is 'polysemic' – they have, by design, many possible meanings, depending on their contexts and modifications by other metaphors, and so they are never reducible into literalistic translations.

However, it must be admitted that I have just done something rather strange with these metaphors. I have thought about them without a more than incidental reference to Jesus of Nazareth. I think it important to do this, because the New Testament insists that we can speak of the Word of God before all creation, and certainly long before the birth of Jesus. Still, it is pretty obvious that we would not have these specific metaphors if people had not believed that Jesus is the Son and Word of God. Some attempt has to be made to relate the eternal Son and Word, one with God and before all creation, to the human person of Jesus, born at a particular time in history.

Using the sort of language I have so far used, we might say that, just as the eternal Word is the expression and communication of the mind of God as God begins the work of creation, so the historical

Jesus is the expression and communication of the mind of God in a specific human form, for the sake of humans on this planet. Jesus is a specific human implementation of the intelligible blue-print for the creation of intelligent life-forms. And Jesus is a direct and immediate expression of the living, active and personal being of God as it turns towards created personal beings on this planet.

For Christians, the world that we see and touch and feel is a world of appearances, dependent on a deeper underlying reality of Spirit, of consciousness, wisdom and beauty. The whole of space and time is an expression, half-revealing and half-veiling, of this time-transcending, eternal reality. Nevertheless, some parts of space and time will be more revelatory, more disclosive of their spiritual core. The existence of a person who appreciates the beauty of the created cosmos reveals more of the nature of God than do millions of light-years of 'empty' space. Some persons, those who are fully alive to the beauty of God's world and to the moral ideal of love that underlies it, disclose God more than others. Christians believe that on this planet, the person of Jesus is so fully a disclosure of God that he is an unveiling of infinite spirit under the forms of time – 'in him all the fullness of God was pleased to dwell' (Col. 1.19).

Jesus, seen simply and solely as a human person, is not the eternal Word and Son. But Jesus expresses the eternal Word and Son as fully as they can be expressed in the context of the human world, in and through a human person. In that sense Jesus 'is' the Word and Son of God, and insofar as he remains in recognizable human form (however transfigured by resurrection that may be) he will remain the Word and Son of God. Or perhaps, given the immense size of the universe, we should say that Jesus will always be the Word and Son of God in human form, since there may be other forms of expression of an infinite Word that we can hardly imagine.

The starting point for much Christian thinking about the relation of Jesus to God has been the statement in the Prologue to John's Gospel: 'The Word became flesh' (John 1.14). The meta-phorical nature of this statement can be brought out by putting it in unfamiliar terms: 'The dictionary entry turned into a lamb chop.' Of course, that is absurd. It carries no spiritual meaning at all. But it makes the point that this is what John's statement might sound like to someone who tried to take it literally.

We begin to put meaning into the statement when we interpret 'the Word' in the light of the story of God's creation, and we see that what is being referred to, in a metaphorical way, is the expression of God's creative will. In a similar way, 'flesh' refers to the material world, and in particular to human beings as parts of the material world. The 'flesh' is often contrasted with the 'spirit', and this is not just contrasting the material with the spiritual. It is thinking of human lives centred on the love of material things, as contrasted with human lives centred on the love of goodness and beauty and on unselfish love of others.

Taking this web of connected meanings together, we can say that God's creative will is definitively expressed in a material and bodily form that has all the typical desires and dispositions of human nature, but is nevertheless wholly directed by the will of God. It is very easy to misinterpret this. The eternal wisdom of God does not change into a human being. It does not change into anything, for it always remains what it eternally is, the living and active wisdom of God (what the Hebrew Bible calls 'the Torah', the eternal pattern of the written words of the revelation given to Moses by God).

For orthodox Jews, the Torah (the books of the Bible from Genesis to Deuteronomy plus the oral laws of God recorded in the Talmud) is an eternal pattern rooted in the mind of God, which is expressed in Hebrew words. For orthodox Christians, the eternal pattern rooted in the mind of God is expressed in one human person, Jesus of Nazareth. The New Testament could have said that Jesus is the Torah of God, as well as the Word and Son of God. Perhaps one reason why it did not is that there already existed a written Torah, and that may have been confusing. But it makes good (metaphorical) sense to say that Jesus is the Torah fully embodied in a person, rather than in a written text.

That is not really too surprising, since God's blueprint for the universe includes the emergence of conscious, free and intelligent persons embodied in material organisms. So this part of the blueprint can be expressed in time precisely in such a person, and thereafter in a society of such persons which can realize one important part of the final goal and purpose that God has in creation.

How, we may ask, can God's creative will and purpose be definitively expressed in a free human person, much less in a society of such persons? The sting lies in the word 'free', for must not free persons be independent of God's will? To make them wholly subservient to God's will would, it seems, be to make them puppets, and so not fully human.

I have a very strong commitment to the importance of human freedom. It is hard to give any defence of evil in the world without attributing the responsibility for much of it to a misuse of human freedom. And it is hard to hold humans responsible for making great efforts to learn and develop their characters through difficult struggle, if God could simply have made them do what God wanted by compelling them to act as God wished.

On the other hand, if humans are always free to do evil and to make mistakes, it is equally hard to see how any humans could be guaranteed to be wholly good, so that they would always act in accordance with God's will. And it is hard to see how any human being could ever be called 'the light' or 'the saviour' of the world, since they might give up or fail at any moment.

There is a real dilemma here. We want Jesus to be human, but we also want Jesus to be our saviour from our human bondage to egoism, hatred and aggression that all humans seem to be locked into. Can we have both?

Theologians have wrestled with this problem over the centuries. In one sense, we could simply say that we see God in Jesus. Jesus' life is wholly surrendered to God, so that God can act fully and decisively in and through him. But theologians have probed more deeply, and what they have generally agreed has been something like this: Jesus is fully human. Like the rest of us humans, he has limited knowledge, normal human desires and a limited amount of physical and mental ability. He has a human will, which works on limited knowledge, based on what he has been taught in his short life, which sees things from the viewpoint of his own temperament, culture and history, and which formulates limited goals that present themselves as real possibilities within his own situation.

But Jesus is also fully divine, he is united to God, one with God in the fullest possible sense. Our wills are distinct from the divine will. We may agree with the divine will or not, and that is up to us. It is our own responsibility, and it is unlikely that we will always agree with the divine will, or even know what it is, most of the time. But Jesus' will, while it is human in nature, is not independent of the divine will. It is the will of God, expressed in and through a human will. When God directs Jesus' human will, God is not controlling the will of another person. It is God who is willing in two different ways at the same time – as the infinite and omniscient creator of the whole universe, and as a limited human consciousness, embodied in an organism in one part of a small planet within the universe.

Is it beyond the power of an infinite God to take a finite form? This would not be a matter of God 'shrinking' to become finite. The infinite God would rather add a new finite mode of consciousness to the non-temporal consciousness that belongs to the eternal divine nature.

We may think that God would experience every consciousness anyway, as part of the divine knowledge. That is true, but God would experience my consciousness, for instance, as the consciousness of another separate being. My consciousness is not God's consciousness, even though God knows all that is going on within it.

The consciousness of Jesus, however, would be the consciousness of God in a human mode of being. This consciousness could never fall away from God, or rebel against God, or set itself in opposition to God. For it would be God's own consciousness. It would be what things looked like to God from a particular human point of view.

Such a human would be a finite manifestation of the infinite God, the human 'image of the invisible God' (Col. 1.15). He would be incapable of sin, though he would feel all those things that incline humans to sin; he would feel the pains that humans feel; he would act in ways limited by the capacities of a human body; and he would be bounded in knowledge by what he experienced and learned in his own culture.

What would be the relation of such a human person to God? The limited human awareness of Jesus would know that it was not omniscient, remembering all that had happened and was happening everywhere in the universe. That would be totally impossible for a human mind. So God would be an 'other' consciousness, and would intend and will things elsewhere in the universe about which the human mind of Jesus would know nothing.

Yet what Jesus wills is what God wills in a human mind. God works in and through Jesus, so that Jesus' human will freely co-operates with the divine will, in such a way that there could be no division between them. And Jesus has, as the Gospels testify, a uniquely constant, intense and uninterrupted sense of the presence of the divine mind, of which his human mind is a finite expression.

In the New Testament, this unique awareness of the divine mind and unique conformity with the divine will is represented as the prayer of Jesus to his 'Father in heaven'. God is not literally a father, a person with a Y chromosome who gave birth to a male child, and who lives in the sky. Heaven is not in space-time at all. It is a different, non-physical form of being, filled with the presence of a completely non-physical God. A non-material father is that spiritual reality from whom our whole material existence originates. To pray to the Father is to cultivate a conscious relationship of dependence and trust with this spiritual source of our being.

In one sense the Father is not different from the Son, since the Son, Jesus, is the finite expression of the infinite source of all things. Yet in another sense the difference could not be greater, since the Son is finite and fallible, while the Father is infinite and omniscient. Jesus' prayers to the heavenly Father sustain the sense of unity with that greater all-enveloping reality which he manifests in a finite way.

John's Gospel says, not that God became flesh, but that the Word, which 'was with God, and was God', became flesh. This expresses a similar sense of both unity and difference. The Word is God, and yet is with God. We have to speak of a diversity-in-unity when we speak of God. The Word is an intelligible, living, active and personal form of divine life. It depends totally upon, is generated from, and is indivisible from, the ultimate spiritual source of all things. Jesus' relationship to God expresses in time the timeless relationship of the Personal Word to the Ultimate Source of all. It is a relationship of dependence, held within a deeper form of unity. So it is the creative and self-expressive wisdom of God that is fully present and active in the human person of Jesus.

In this profound sense Jesus is unique among human beings. Yet we need always to bear in mind that saying that Jesus is the Word or the Son of God, though it is true, is a metaphorical statement with many levels of meaning. To put it in a more traditional way, it is a 'mystery', a truth of faith that cannot be put in a straightforwardly literal and readily comprehensible way.

Metaphors of atonement

Jesus is the image of the invisible God. He is also the Saviour, the liberator of created human wills from hatred, greed and pride, and the one who unites fallen human wills to the divine will. This is atonement – making humans and God 'at-one'.

Christians see the human condition as one of estrangement from God. Humans do not know God clearly and they do not obey God's will easily. The human world is one that is always prone to greed, selfishness, violence and uncontrolled desire. In his letter to the Christians in Rome, Paul quotes Psalm 14: 'There is no one who is righteous, not even one . . . all have turned aside, together they have become worthless' (Rom. 3.10–12).

That is a severe judgement, but it is largely confirmed by the terrible narrative of wars, slavery and oppression that makes up most of human history. If the human world is to return to God, to love, selflessness and justice, it may well seem that only God could bring that about by some action that could reconcile estranged humanity to God. Christians believe that 'in Christ God was reconciling the world to himself' (2 Cor. 5.19). The atonement is God's entrance into an estranged world in Jesus to make that world 'at-one' with the divine mind and will.

The world became estranged from God because God created free and autonomous agents who must be truly distinct from God. They must therefore have the possibility of choosing to follow selfish desires instead of learning love. There must be the possibility of realizing such selfish desires, with all the consequences of conflict and the oppression of the innocent that is implied. If human agents live in communities of relationship, and if their choices carry causal significance for the future, then the human world cannot be completely determined by God alone.

God may will and may enable humans to choose the good. But if humans are to be free, God must permit them to choose against the good, to destroy positive relationships, and to bring about states that conflict with the will of God. The cosmos must carry within it the possibility of destruction and evil, and if that possibility is realized, the world will be alienated from the will and presence of God.

Maybe it is in some deep sense necessary that God should create the sorts of good and beautiful things that can only exist in a created universe which contains free and partly self-shaping creatures. Yet it may also be necessary that possibilities of destruction and evil are inseparable from such a free and autonomous creation.

God said, 'Let there be light' (Gen. 1.3). God saw that the light was good, and separated the light from the darkness. Yet light carries darkness with it, as night follows day. So, when God intends the good, that intention inevitably carries with it the possibility of its absence, of evil, of that which is its opposite. And this is not just a bare possibility. 'I form light and create darkness,' says the Lord, 'I make weal and create woe' (Isa. 45.7). 'Good things and bad, life and death, poverty and wealth, come from the Lord . . . error and darkness were created with sinners' (Sirach 11.14–16). The ordered cosmos itself was shaped from a formless void (Gen. 1.1 and Wisdom 11.17), from the great sea which hovers at the edges of order, the chaos out of which the bounded world is formed.

In these cryptic texts scattered throughout the Old Testament lies the thought that chaos and darkness itself is created, like Leviathan, the great serpent of the deep (Isa. 27.1), who will be slain only on the final Day of the Lord, when the story of our cosmos comes to an end. Why should such things be created?

The book of Job is the Bible's answer to that question. But it is a book in which every answer given by human reason is rejected, and it ends with the voice of God out of the whirlwind: 'Where were you when I laid the foundation of the earth? Tell me, if you have understanding' (Job 38.4).

There is no one correct interpretation of Job. But for me this is a poetic way of talking of the utter transcendence of God. It means that the creator of the cosmos is not just another finite but very powerful being, who happens to have the nature he has, though he might have been quite different or might even not have existed, who is just there by chance. God is the one and only source of all beings, and is beyond all beings. God is the self-existent abyss from which all beings spring. God alone must be, and cannot be other than God is.

So we cannot think of God as children might do, as a person who wonders what he might create, who draws up a number of proposals, and then decides to create this cosmos. God alone cannot fail to be, and to God's existence and nature there is no alternative. God must be as God is; but necessity is not a constraint or limitation on God. It is the inner character of Being itself, containing in itself the potentiality of all finite forms of being, yet itself without bounds or limitations, the unbounded ocean of Being. That, for me, is what Job saw when he finally saw God and confessed: 'I have uttered what I did not understand' (Job 42.3).

Yet the prophetic tradition that culminated in Jesus increasingly saw that the necessity of God is also and primarily a necessity of love, for 'God is love' (1 John 4.8). It is not a necessity that proceeds blindly, without creative spontaneity and personal responsiveness. For what is necessary is precisely that love should be creative and spontaneous, and that it should relate to others in ways that respect their freedom and nourish their own self-unfolding.

Since our world springs from the necessity of God, we must say of it, 'It must be.' But since our world springs from the creative love of God, we must also say, 'What must be is a world in which freedom is possible, and in which freedom can be fulfilled in love.'

God creates the darkness. But God does not will the darkness. God wills a world in which darkness must be, because without it there could be no creatures compounded of darkness and light. We are such creatures. The second Genesis creation story puts it in metaphorical but profound form: 'God formed man from the dust of the ground' (Gen. 2.7). Humans, beings of dust, were placed in a garden. But the garden was surrounded by wilderness. In it was a forbidden tree, and a serpent who tempted the humans to disobey God. The theme is repeated in Job, when Satan, 'the Accuser', has the task of testing and tempting humans (Job 1.12).

These stories express the thought that humans emerge from, and are parts of, the material world. That world has the essential possibility of turning from God, and there is a real temptation to do so. That is how the world, even in its presumed original goodness, is constituted.

With the modern scientific understanding of how all things in the universe are entangled or interconnected, and of how new emergent realities (for instance, heavy atoms) are formed by vast destructive forces (supernovae), we can see more clearly how destruction and creation go together in the structure of our universe. We can see how our universe could not produce the complex carbon-based life-forms it does unless its basic laws and constants were exactly what they are. So we at least begin to see how darkness and light, chaos and order, both essentially exist in the formation of our emergent, partly self-shaping, interconnected cosmos.

If we ask why the cosmos should be thus, then we can say that we, as carbon-based intelligences (minds generated from dust), could not exist in any other universe than this. Yet we have freedom to share in God's creativity and compassion or to follow the way of self-centred desire and indifference to others. Humans have long ago made their choice, and the Gospel of John says, 'This is the judgement, that the light has come into the world, and people loved darkness rather than light' (John 3.19).

Suffering increases exponentially, as human violence, greed and the will to power make actual the possibilities of evil and destruction that have always existed as possibilities in the structure of our world. God has not willed that, and the prophets roundly condemn it: 'Should you not know justice? – you who hate the good and love the evil . . . they will cry to the LORD, but he will not answer them; he will hide his face from them . . . because they have acted wickedly' (Mic. 3.1–4).

So we must distinguish between what God creates by necessity (without which there could be no material, emergent, free, self-shaping, social agents) and what God creates by intention and design (a society of creative and compassionate intelligences raised from the dust of long-dead stars). The evil that happens to men and women is not what God does to them. It is what comes upon them in a world alienated and estranged from God, from which God 'hides his face'. Such a world has turned towards the dark. The waters of chaos have been released, and even the innocent are caught in the flood, and cry, 'O LORD, do not be far away! O my help, come quickly to my aid!' (Ps. 22.19).

The gospel of Christ is that God enters into the broken world, to bring healing and the hope of deliverance. It was Jesus of Nazareth who said, 'He has sent me to proclaim release to the captives, and recovery of sight to the blind, to let the oppressed go free, to proclaim the year of the Lord's favour' (Luke 4.18–19). We humans are imprisoned by obsessive desire, blind to the glory of God, oppressed by the brutalities we inflict on one another, and enslaved by the anxieties of a life without ultimate hope.

God's love is not something that prevents the occurrence of suffering. Even God cannot do that. Some suffering is necessary in any material cosmos like ours, and the vast majority of suffering is the consequence of human enslavement to chaos and desire, which consequence even God cannot prevent. God's love is a love that has a positive moral goal for creation, that offers liberation from both suffering and self-centred desire, and promises that the goal will be realized, so that nothing in our disordered lives need be in vain or pointless. Even the darkest moment, even the death of the incarnate Word of God as a criminal in the agony of the cross, can be given significant meaning in the overall pattern of the human story. And that meaning is not just for others, or for the world in general. It is a meaning that can lead to an infinite value for each human soul, for those who suffer and for those who have made them suffer, on the one condition of free acceptance of the gracious love of God.

God's love is seen by Christians supremely in the person of Jesus, who endures evil and attains the goal God sets for human fulfilment. In his own person, Jesus takes humanity into the life of God. He opens the door to eternal life in a world that has become estranged from God. So he becomes not only the incarnation of God in human life, but also the liberating Saviour of the human world, re-uniting it to its supreme spiritual source and goal.

Many Christians find the focus of their devotion to Jesus in the symbol of the cross, which helps them to think of Jesus as the Saviour who died in order to take away sin, who by his passion and death enabled sin to be forgiven and made companionship with God possible. I can see the attraction of that. The thought that someone has given their life that I may live, and has 'paid the price' of my wrong-doing on my behalf, is moving and powerful. But it is only one of many images in the New Testament for how it is that God has entered into the suffering human world in order to unite us to the divine life.

For me, it has the disadvantage that it concentrates on some negative aspects of the gospel – on suffering and death, on my consciousness of sin and guilt, and on the necessity for some price to be paid to God before God can forgive us. I do not deny that such aspects exist. Suffering and death are real, and to say that God shares in them is to say something profound and tragic about human life and about God. My wrong-doing is real, and it does merit some form of penalty, some cost to me of the failed human life I have made for myself. To say that Christ, by his death, pays that penalty for me can produce a deep sense of gratitude and relief.

Nonetheless, the positive Christian gospel is a gospel of joy, happiness, freedom and new life. The suffering of God on the cross is followed by the joy of resurrection and by the gift of new life in the Spirit. So the cross is for me not best concentrated on as a place of pain and sorrow, but rather as the door to eternal life and joy. 'Unless a grain of wheat falls into the earth and dies, it remains just a single grain; but if it dies, it bears much fruit' (John 12.24).

The death of Jesus is necessary, this world being what it is; for evil seeks to destroy goodness. But it is not the death alone that redeems humanity. It is the self-offering of life, and because it is divine life it triumphs over death, and is given to those who ask. The cross is not, in my view, some sort of penalty that I should have endured but allow someone else to endure instead. We do not have to think in terms of penalties and punishments at all. We can think instead of our human situation as one of desolation, violence and tragic suffering. We can think of God entering into this desolate world, healing, loving and acting with compassion, but being rejected and killed – not as a penalty, but as a tragic example of innocent goodness exterminated by human malevolence. Yet if that was all that happened, then Jesus' life and mission would have been a failure.

The positive gospel is precisely that goodness was not exterminated. It became a powerful force in human history, as Christ was raised to glory and the Spirit of Christ was released into the lives of men and women. The 'atonement', the making-one, of God and humanity is found in the completed triptych of death, resurrection and spiritual indwelling. Human sin is forgiven, wiped away, as the Spirit of Christ transfigures the human heart. It is not that some external penalty has been remitted, leaving me otherwise just what I was before. My whole life has been changed, made anew, by the power of the Spirit.

There may still be a process I must undergo to make amends for my wrong-doings. But I am assured of unity with God, because it is God – the same God who suffered and died on the cross, and who took humanity into the divine life – who has united me to himself in and through Christ's self-sacrificial and glorified life.

From this perspective, it may well seem that some Christian spirituality has been unduly negative, in focusing too much on sin, on penalty, on guilt and on suffering, whereas the focus can be mainly on new life, on transfiguration, on love and on freedom. Probably we need both. That is why there are many images of atonement and redemption in the New Testament – images of liberation from slavery, of victory over evil, and of healing from disease, as well as images of remission of penalty (I have discussed images of the atonement in more detail in *What the Bible Really Teaches*, chapter 7).

We should not forget that, in the end, Good Friday is 'Good', not because on that day a man died in agony, but because on that day God gave up the human life he had assumed, in order to raise to eternal joy all human lives that would respond positively to that divine self-emptying.

Metaphors of salvation

The heart of the Christian idea of atonement is that in Jesus humanity and divinity are united, and that we can be included in this unity by the dynamic energy of the Spirit. The Spirit 'sanctifies' human lives, uniting them ever more closely to God until they attain final salvation, the fullness of health and well-being that lies in completed conscious unity with God.

This has been put in terms of classical Christian theology by saying that the eternal Son and the human personhood of Jesus are two 'natures' united in one 'person'. They are united, the Council of Chalcedon said in AD 451, without being confused and yet without division. Yet these terms are not to be found anywhere in the Bible. So, while not denying their helpfulness for those who can think in terms of Greek philosophy, it may be helpful to look at the way the New Testament puts the central idea of divine–human unity in and through Jesus.

Most of what it says on this subject is found in John's Gospel. According to John, Jesus said, 'I am in the Father and the Father is in me' (John 14.11). At once we are firmly in the land of metaphor. Jesus is not spatially 'inside' the Father, and the Father is not spatially inside Jesus. The first rule of metaphor is met – the statement is not literally true. The second rule is also met – it is not at all clear what Jesus and the Father being 'in' one another means, and different people have interpreted it in different ways. The third rule asks us to look at other similar metaphors of 'being in someone' in other biblical texts, and see if that casts any light on the matter.

It is not long before we come across other uses of this spatial metaphor of one thing being 'in' another. Jesus says to his disciples, 'Abide in me as I abide in you' (John 15.4). Paul says, 'the Spirit of God dwells in you' (Rom. 8.9), and 'Christ is in you' (8.10). Paul also says, 'As in Adam all die, in Christ all will be made alive' (1 Cor. 15.22, NIV).

Perhaps the easiest of these to grasp is that the Spirit lives in you. The Christian life consists largely in letting the Spirit of God act in us. The Spirit of God is referred to in the Genesis creation story. When the earth was formless and void, and darkness covered the deep, 'the spirit of God swept over the face of the waters' (Gen. 1.2, NRSV alternative translation). The Spirit of God is like a mighty wind – in fact the Hebrew words can mean 'a mighty wind', yet another metaphor for God's creative being. The image is of a dark and deep abyss, an unbounded sea of pure possibility, an infinite sea touched by the wind of the divine Spirit.

The Spirit, like the Word, both is God and is with God. It is not other than God. It is the primal breath of God, a wind that is terrifying in its irresistible power and refreshing in its cooling touch. This is not God in utter transcendence, the silent source beyond all thought. It is not God in intelligible beauty, the intricate and ordered pattern of all finite worlds. It is God in creative energy and life-giving power, driving over the darkness of chaos to form it and shape it into a moving image of eternal Beauty.

God is the origin, the intelligible form and the dynamic life of all things. God speaks the creative Word, and the Spirit forms that Word in the material world. When God says, 'Let us make humankind in our image' (Gen. 1.26), it is the primordial Father, the self-expressive Word, and the dynamically creative Spirit who speak. They speak together as one, for they are one. Their unity is beyond isolated and unrelated being, and beyond a plurality of many minds and wills. It is unity and relationship in inextricable and dialectical interplay. The Lord our God is one. But that primal unity includes within itself a diversity of ways of being. As it turns towards the world in its creative activity, we understand it as Father and source of all, as the intelligible pattern of all that is, and as the creative energy that gives life and being to all things.

Thus Paul says that, as the Spirit moved over the waters of chaos, so it moves within us to give life and authentic being to us. Amid all the chaos and possibility of our lives, we need the action of the Spirit to give form and shape to what we do, and to make actual those possibilities that are in us but that we may be unable or unwilling to realize.

When we act, we intend to do something and we initiate the action that will bring it about (or at least we think we do). If the Spirit acts, then the Spirit intends and initiates actions. This can sound like a spiritual take-over, when I sit back and let another agent form intentions in my mind and initiate actions through my body. I become an instrument for someone else's intentions and actions, rather like being someone hypnotized.

Perhaps the idea of 'co-operation' fits the case better. I try to let my intentions be influenced by God, and I actively try to become a channel of God's love. There is another source of agency working through my mind, but I have to let it work and actively co-operate with it.

Such causal agency is 'within' me, because it is not imposed from without or by any visible agent outside my body. God works in my mind, causing thoughts to arise and acts to be initiated. I remain an agent, responsible for my acts. But I freely co-operate with a causal agency that can influence my mind in various ways. On this account, the 'Spirit living within me' would mean that God continually exercises a co-operative causal influence directly on my mind, insofar as I allow God to do so.

In the passages quoted, Paul uses 'Christ' and 'the Spirit' interchangeably. This draws attention to their deep unity. The Spirit is not just a power sent from God; it is God in creative co-operation with human hearts and minds. For Christians the Spirit has become the Spirit of Christ. That is because it took definitive form in the person of Jesus, and the life of Jesus is for us the pattern of the present inward activity of the Spirit. To live in the Spirit is the highest ideal of the Christian life. That is not just any spirit. It is the Spirit that filled the life of Jesus, and took definitive form in him. So we can say that Christ is the pattern of our lives, and the Spirit is the power of our lives. So we distinguish Son and Spirit, and that reflects a sort of distinction in God.

The distinction, as we understand it, is expressed in metaphors rooted in history, in the life of Jesus, but referring to the supreme mystery of God. We should never say that we completely comprehend it, in specific detail. Yet it is reasonable to say that these metaphors enable us to picture it in a way that is not misleading, as long as we are alive to the shifting, complex and diverse meanings of metaphor, and as long as we do not think either that metaphors are literal truths or that they are no more than poetic imaginings that do not state truths at all.

But can 'living in Christ' mean, in an exactly similar way, that I exercise a co-operative causal influence on the mind of Christ? Well, not in an exactly similar way, since Christ is the expression of the infinite and eternal God, and I am not. I am not going to influence God's intentions and actions. Or am I?

If God acts throughout the whole universe, and in many human minds, any influence I have on God will be minute. It is certainly not going to change the master-plan that God has for the whole universe, or the way that God acts throughout the whole range of space and time. Still, I may make a small difference to the precise way God acts in this small part of the universe, and to the particular purposes God has for the day-to-day lives of the people I know and meet.

To 'live in Christ' is to be part of a much larger active purpose and will. When 'Christ is in me', Christ is not a small part of me. On the contrary, Christ works inwardly (without external bodily stimuli) through me, but also works through other people and through things in the world at large. I am part of a larger will and purpose. As I do, or fail to do, God's will, I may cause God to re-formulate the divine purposes to take account of my tiny actions. And, as I seek to co-operate with God, I may, by my tiny creative contributions, give a specific form to God's actions in my bit of the world.

So I live in Christ insofar as I try to be part of the healing activity of God in the world, and Christ lives in me insofar as God acts directly on my mind to inspire me to new thoughts and acts. We can say that Christ lives in the Father insofar as he consciously expresses God's activity in the world, and the Father lives in Christ insofar as God directs his thoughts and acts. The two expressions look at first as though they are saying something contradictory – two different things are each inside the other, which is impossible. But if we see them as pointing to God's activity mediated through and fully expressed in a finite person who is fully aware of and freely co-operative with that activity, then both expressions can be true at the same time.

But now the difference between Jesus Christ and other humans – that he alone is the Word of God – seems to have been qualified. Is it not just a matter of degree that the Word is fully expressed in Jesus, and that Jesus is fully aware of God's acts in him, while God acts in us, and we are aware of God, to a lesser degree? There is indeed an important spiritual truth here. Christians are to 'live in Christ', and if Christ is the Word of God, and we live in Christ, then we must in some sense be parts of the divine Word. Yet there remains an immense difference. 'Living in Christ' is something we try, and very often fail, to achieve. We always remain prone to sin, and it is only by the grace of God that we are counted as living in Christ more fully than we actually do. But Jesus always and at every moment was the unqualified expression of the eternal Word. That is rather more than a matter of degree. We, all of us, are more or less good, but Jesus is absolutely perfect, wholly without sin.

Between the intermittently and the more-or-less good and the perfect there is a dimensional difference. That is why we might revere some human beings, but we worship Jesus Christ alone. They are trying, by God's help, to be good, to be fulfilled human beings. Jesus is the standard of human goodness and fulfilment. He is the human image of perfect beauty and goodness, and as such he can be the object of unqualified devotion, for he is the definitive and God-ordained finite image of Infinite Goodness. As the New Testament puts it, he is the Son by nature, and we are sons and daughters by adoption and grace (Gal. 4.4–7).

Christian faith is not just believing that a set of historical events happened a long time ago. The death and resurrection of Jesus could be seen just as objective historical events, and no more. But they would then lack religious significance. Christian faith is dying with Christ, renouncing selfish desires, and being raised to share in the life of Christ here and now. It is an attempted renunciation of self and an acceptance of the renewing life of God through the Spirit. It is living 'in Christ', in a community which is constituted by the action of the Spirit, expressed through the sacraments of the Church. The Spirit is patterned on and defined by the life of

Jesus, who was the Spirit's decisive and normative historical manifestation. Jesus' life 'saves' us, because it is the pattern for and the historical origin of the dynamic action of the Spirit which liberates from sin and unites to God in the fellowship of the Church, the continuing 'body of Christ'.

What I have been doing in Part 3 is exploring how biblically rooted metaphors form the basis for the development of Christian faith in a threefold God who is the creator, saviour and sanctifier of finite human persons in a world estranged from its creator. It cannot plausibly be said that the developed Christian view is explicitly set out in a systematic way in the Bible. The Bible is more like a source of metaphors that can be patterned in a number of different ways, and placed within diverse philosophical frameworks or world-views. Modern biblical scholarship helps us to see how these metaphors have developed in the Bible, and how they elude any one final literal interpretation.

A central key to reading the Bible after critical enquiry has done its work is to have a vivid sense of the importance of metaphorical language, of its richness, mystery and diversity. If we have a more poetic, sensitive approach to the way in which metaphors can give spiritual insight into the infinite reality of God, we will overcome the fear that questioning literal interpretations somehow undermines the objective truth of the biblical texts.

Part 4

THE NEW TESTAMENT

The positive gospel of unlimited divine love

If Jesus' life and teaching is the normative divine revelation of moral goodness, and the key to interpreting all particular texts in the Bible, then many parts of the Bible must be seen as unduly vindictive or judgemental, when judged in the light of Jesus' teaching. We have seen how this is true of some Old Testament passages, which call for harsh punitive treatment of criminals or enemies. But even when biblical criticism has prepared us for seeing some parts of the Bible as expressing very limited or even mistaken human discernments of God's nature and will, we may still be surprised to find such limitations in the New Testament. But it is not really so surprising. For the disciples and Gospel editors did not necessarily have a full understanding of Jesus' message and of its implications, even as they set out to record it.

For example, Matthew's Gospel is in many ways a rather judgemental Gospel. It speaks of divine judgement, of 'weeping and gnashing of teeth', much more than any other Gospel. It is in Matthew that we read that, at the Judgement, 'These [i.e. those who did not feed the hungry, welcome strangers or visit the sick] will go away into eternal punishment [*kolasin aionion*]' (Matt. 25.46). You could read that as a proof that there is an eternal punishment in hell, from which there will be no escape. Note, however, that those punished are not unbelievers, or those who reject belief in Jesus as their Saviour. They are the morally unconcerned, regardless of what they believe.

If this is truly part of inspired Scripture, then it is something we must take seriously. There are real and painful consequences of not caring for others. But there are good scriptural reasons for not taking it literally. A main one lies in Jesus' repeated teaching of unlimited forgiveness: '[You should forgive] not seven times, but, I tell you, seventy-seven times' (Matt. 18.22). It would be absurd to say that you should not forgive on the seventy-eighth occasion. The obvious meaning is that you should forgive without limit. But God cannot be less forgiving than human beings, so it follows that God will forgive without limit. How is that consistent with God giving eternal punishments?

It is not! There are many ways of making these two texts consistent. The one that appeals to me is that 'eternal punishment' is to be interpreted, like 'eternal life', primarily as a quality of life. Just as eternal life is life with the eternal God, so eternal punishment, or eternal death, is life without the eternal God, a life of exclusion from God, with a full realization of how self-destructive that is.

But will it go on for ever, without any hope of escape? If God's forgiveness is unlimited, and if repentance is possible for any soul, then we can escape from eternal punishment if we sincerely repent, just as we can escape from 'eternal fire' if we repent. The fire, the punishment, remains as a timeless possibility. But since God endured even the cross to procure our forgiveness, it seems that God will not let death separate anyone wholly from divine love: 'love is strong as death' (Song of Sol. 8.6). God's love remains changeless. I think that means that, even if we are judged wanting and sent to a timeless state of seeming separation from God, God will still be there ('If I make my bed in Sheol [the place of the dead], you are there': Ps. 139.8). God will still accept us if we sincerely turn to God.

So no-one is condemned to hell, to eternal punishment, without hope of release. There is judgement; there is the self-inflicted torture of fully realizing that we have put ourselves into a loveless, Godless, world. There is no limit to that unhappy state; it is 'ageless', without a temporal limit. Yet even there the hope of redemption exists, for God's love, shown to us in Jesus Christ, cannot be limited by anything in creation. Even the dead can be saved by faith. No-one can guarantee that they will be; but no Christian may deny that they can be. And perhaps Christians should pray for that.

If we read the texts about judgement and the 'flames' and 'outer darkness' out of context and in isolation, we may come to believe that God will torture people for ever because of what they have done in a few short years on earth. But if we read such texts in the light of the gospel of God's unlimited love for all creation, we will have to deny that God would torture anyone, or that God would ever close the door of salvation to anyone. If there is a place of punishment, it is one we freely enter, where we suffer the consequences of our own hatreds and selfish passions. And it is a place from which God, who desires the salvation of all, desires and will open the possibility for our release.

How do we know that unlimited love and forgiveness is a higher or better insight than endless punishment? Because the nature of God's love is revealed on the cross, and in Jesus' life of forgiveness and healing. That is the test by which Scripture itself must be judged.

Without Scripture, we probably would not know of Jesus' sacrifice to 'take away the sin of the world' (John 1.29). The Scripture records these beliefs at an early date, when Jesus' death and resurrection were still vividly remembered by those who had seen them. So Scripture is vitally important as the record of the remembered acts of God in Christ. There is every reason to think that the record is reliable, since it springs from groups who experienced the risen Christ as a living presence among them, and who learned about Jesus from those who had known recent witnesses of Jesus' life and resurrection. But there is little reason to think that there will be no errors or limitations of understanding in Scripture, since the records are by human beings who interpreted what they had seen in the light of their own beliefs and expectations. What we have to do, therefore, is to seek out the most morally and spiritually mature insights in Scripture, and use those as the standard by which to assess the rest.

When we do that, we will probably find that there are places which seem hardly to grasp the full impact of Jesus' teaching at all, even though that teaching is clearly recorded elsewhere. The Gospels themselves record instances of such failures on the part of the Apostles. Luke records that when one town rejected Jesus' teaching, James and John wanted to call down fire from heaven to destroy the town (Luke 9.51–56). But Jesus rebuked them, and some ancient authorities record Jesus as saying, 'You do not know what spirit you are of, for the Son of Man has not come to destroy the lives of human beings, but to save them.' Luke also records that an argument broke out among the Apostles as to who was the greatest (Luke 9.46–48). But Jesus said, 'The least among all of you is the greatest.' It seems that even the Apostles were sometimes ambitious and vindictive. They sometimes failed to see the impact of Jesus' teaching that worldly triumph and the destructive punishment of others are opposed to God's will and purpose.

From these passages we learn that the earthly triumph of the Church through the use of force, and the destructive punishment of others, is not compatible with Jesus' teaching. Despite this, a letter by Paul or one of his followers states that there will be a time, quite soon (that was two thousand years ago!) when 'the Lord Jesus is revealed from heaven with his mighty angels in flaming fire, inflicting vengeance on those who do not know God, and on those who do not obey the gospel of our Lord Jesus' (2 Thess. 1.7, 8). The writer obviously did not know 'what spirit he was of'. Jesus will not come with flaming fire to take vengeance on non-Christians. Jesus will not come to destroy lives, but to save them. For that very reason, he will not come as soon as the writer thought (within a generation), for millions as yet unborn have not yet had the chance of salvation. But God will give them that chance.

If we hold fast to a clear conviction that Jesus comes to save the world, and not to condemn it (John 3.17), then we will know that vindictive thoughts, like that of Jesus sending unbelievers to eternal destruction, are completely opposed to the gospel – which is good news for all, not bad news for many.

What, then, are we to make of passages like that in the second letter to the Thessalonians? We are certainly not to take them as true! We are to take the Thessalonians passage as one man's expectation, his way of understanding what the final making-present of Christ in glory would be like. Because Jesus' resurrection had taken place, he thought the general resurrection and the end of history would come soon. And because evil was still rampant in the world, and Christians were being persecuted, he thought that the persecutors would get what they deserved, and be persecuted.

There was something right in what he thought. Jesus had been raised from death, and human history does have an ultimate goal, which is that all things should be united in Christ (Eph. 1.10). Evil will then be wholly destroyed, and all who have done evil will have to face up to what they have done. But he has misunderstood two very important things. He has misunderstood the breadth of God's love, which wills that there should be untold millions of humans who can be included in the plan of salvation, which will accordingly take a much longer time than one generation. And he has misunderstood the depth of God's love, which does not wreak vindictive vengeance on anyone, but 'desires everyone to be saved' (1 Tim. 2.4). Eternal destruction is a warning of what our ultimate state will be if we persist in hatred and egoism. But God stands ready to redeem any who at any time accept the divine love.

What this passage tells us, then, is how even firmly committed disciples can misunderstand God's love, and turn it into something limited and judgemental, while the teaching of Christ is that God's love is unlimited and redemptive. It is a lesson in human short-sightedness and our capacity for a triumphalist and vindictive sort of belief in God ('We might look like losers now; but we will win, and you will all be very sorry'). It is a warning of the dangers of faith, and a reminder that faith without love, without the putting-aside of all triumphalist and vindictive thoughts, is opposed to Christ's teaching. That, in fact, is what the apparently rather vindictive parable of the Last Judgement, the sheep and the goats, in Matthew 25, is all about. Faith is not enough. It is the believers who will get a big surprise at Judgement Day, when they are told they are big hairy goats, while the people without faith, but with love, will be nice woolly sheep. Of course, what God wants is both faith and love. We must be very sure that our faith excludes no-one from love, and that God's love is infinitely deeper and more extensive than any human love could ever be. Only if we keep a very firm grasp on that will we read the Bible aright.

God inspires the thoughts of those who try to witness to the gospel. But it seems that sometimes God is working with extremely resistant material, and the witness turns out to be very alarming for most of the population. Perhaps the Christian message should be: never adopt a judgemental or vindictive attitude, which condemns the sins of others without seeking to understand what may have made them what they are, and help them to see what is truly good. Always hold out the hope and the promise of wider and deeper love, wisdom and understanding. That is the positive gospel.

Metaphors of the kingdom of God

An objection to this sort of account of the gospel is that the first
Christians believed that the world would end soon with a cataclys-
mic judgement, that only a small remnant would be saved, and
that there would at any moment be a miraculous institution of a
new world order. Some early Christians did indeed believe this.
The letters to the Thessalonians look for the return of Christ in
glory, bringing judgement on evil and salvation for believers,
within a generation (1 Thess. 4.15; 2 Thess. 1.6–10). Even here,
however, the most important beliefs are that evil will be judged
and eventually eliminated, and that Christ will be revealed in glory,
and will unite all those of faith to God for ever. Yet when these
beliefs are given a historical placing, the time-scale is all wrong.

But put yourself in the situation of the biblical writers. They
had no idea of a long evolutionary history, or of the amazing
technological advances that would become possible on earth. They
saw a world of warring empires, in which the Hebrew prophets
foretold judgement on oppressors and a future of peace for Israel.
They saw Israel as groaning under Roman domination, but they
also saw the Roman Empire as already beginning to fray at the
edges. This was a time when Rome might be defeated, and Israel
be renewed and take her rightful place as a proud and respected
nation. It was into this volatile context that Jesus was born, and in
which he began to teach about the kingdom of God. But what
exactly was his message?

Jesus is portrayed in the Gospels as a young man who gathered
around him a group of disciples, 12 of them in particular being
commissioned to proclaim Jesus' message of national repentance,
because the 'kingdom of God' had drawn near (this is what the
Greek verb *engiken* means).

Strange as it may seem, scholars are not agreed on what exactly
was meant by this message. One interpretation, the literalist one,

is that Jesus thought that human history was coming to an end, and that God would miraculously intervene to establish a Jewish kingdom in which the Torah would be perfectly obeyed. This interpretation, even though it was held by Albert Schweitzer, seems unduly pedestrian, given the highly metaphorical and elliptical nature of much of Jesus' recorded teaching. Frankly, it also seems too crudely materialistic and nationalistic for a great spiritual teacher. If that was what Jesus thought, he was also just plain wrong, which is something of an embarrassment for present-day Christians.

At the other end of the spectrum of interpretations, the kingdom of God is given a wholly spiritual meaning. It is taken by the great German scholar Adolf von Harnack to refer to the rule of God in the hearts of men and women, not at all to a national Jewish state. Jesus is teaching that God can rule in the heart, and his message is primarily one of moral renewal and of an inner acceptance of the transforming Spirit of God. This has the advantage of being a profound spiritual message. But it also seems to omit important Christian themes like the importance of Jesus' death and resurrection, the urgency of the message for Israel's future, the promise of his rule 'for ever' as Davidic King of Israel, and the hope for a coming of the Son of Man in power and glory.

One important clue to Jesus' meaning can be found by comparing Jesus' gospel with one of the earliest statements of the gospel of the early Church: 'Christ died for our sins in accordance with the scriptures . . . he was buried, and was raised on the third day' (1 Cor. 15.3). This was not Jesus' own message, and could only have been preached after his death. It contains three vital elements. First, Jesus gave his life because of human sin, and in order to liberate humans from the power of sin. Second, he thereby fulfilled the prophetic teaching that God's chosen servant would liberate humans from evil and establish the reign of God. And third, after his death he appeared to his disciples to assure humans of the possibility of eternal life with God.

What a purely spiritual interpretation of the kingdom omits is any sense of historical decisiveness. Jesus could be seen as a great spiritual teacher indeed, but if that is all he is, then what he teaches is what any spiritual teacher could in principle teach, the nearness of God and the possibility of personal devotion to God. Those are important spiritual themes. But was God doing something unique, new and decisive in Jesus? Was God doing something historically specific that would liberate humans from evil, and was God raising Jesus to rule in the kingdom?

This is where the doctrines of the incarnation and the resurrection become important. If Jesus was more than a prophet, if Jesus was God incarnate, then his life and death actually bring about a union of human and divine natures. That (for Christians) is true human liberation, a fulfilment beyond even the dreams of the ancient Hebrew prophets. If Jesus, by his resurrection and Ascension, took humanity into the life of God, then God transforms humanity and rules transfigured human lives in a way that infinitely transcends any form of national or political rule.

This does not mean that liberation was impossible before the life and death of Jesus, or that humans can be alive with God only after the time of Jesus. Abraham, after all, was 'the friend of God'. Elijah was taken up into heaven. Jesus met and talked with Moses and Elijah on the mount of transfiguration. After Jesus' death, he preached to the 'spirits in prison', in *Sheol*, the world of the dead, so they were obviously able to hear and see him in some sense.

What it means is more subtle. Humans can only be liberated and live in God in virtue of the fact that, at one specific point in time, God was incarnate in Jesus, gave his human life in pain, and raised it to glory. God's act happens at a specific place and time, but what is accomplished, its effects, the unity of human and divine in love, is not limited to that place and time. Nor are the effects limited to those who happen to hear about them after they occurred (those to whom the gospel is physically preached).

That is one of the gravest misunderstandings of the nature of salvation, which completely betrays the limitless nature of God's redemptive act in Christ. The effects of God's saving act in Christ reverberate throughout space and time, and are not limited by the laws of ordinary physical influence. So we can say that Abraham was saved by Christ's death and resurrection, even though it was yet to happen, and Abraham did not know of it. For God's will and intention that it should happen was already certain when the first human being came into existence.

If God had not become incarnate then no human would ever have been saved. But God's decree to become incarnate was eternal, 'before' all time, and the salvation the incarnation makes possible extends to every space and time.

Does it, then, matter if we physically hear the gospel or not? Of course it matters. It is better to know the truth than not to know it. More than that, only if you know the truth about God will you be rightly related to God. If you do not know the truth about God, then your knowledge of God, and therefore your relation to God, will be relatively imperfect and incomplete. Of course, that implies that, since none of us know the full truth about God, all of us are incompletely related to God. There will be much to learn in heaven, for all of us! But if we at least know that the love of God is as it is seen in Jesus, and that the Spirit of Christ is the pathway to God, then we have a head start. More importantly, we already have a foretaste of that eternal joy that is ours when we are united in God through the eternal Christ that was embodied in Jesus.

Armed with this understanding of the early-church gospel, which is likely to be closely related to Jesus' own gospel, we can look back at Jesus' message. Jesus urgently called for repentance, and said that the kingdom 'had drawn' near. We can now see the urgency as lying in the necessity for a choice between armed revolt against Rome and an inward turning of the heart to God. The choice would have momentous consequences, and rejection of Jesus' message would mean destruction for the kingdom of Israel. Nevertheless, the kingdom of God had drawn near, precisely in the person of Jesus, who was the anointed king. It was already present to his hearers, and it was to have a critical manifestation with his death and resurrection – though the exact form this would take was unclear to his disciples, and may well have been unclear to Jesus himself. The 'old age' (not the whole of human history) was to come to an end, and a new age was to begin, in which God's kingdom would be near at hand, present in a new but hidden and ambiguous way. But it was not yet clear how God's final purpose would be wholly fulfilled, evil eradicated from the cosmos for ever, and how goodness would be sovereign and uncontested.

In speaking of such things, the metaphors of Apocalyptic writings were used, strange and visionary writings that speak of the end of time, the intermingling of time and eternity, the ultimate battle of good and evil, and the triumph of God's purpose for the cosmos through the death and transfiguration of human hearts and minds. These Apocalyptic texts begin with the book of Daniel, and the symbolism of Apocalypse (the word means 'revelation') is found in many prophetic writings. It develops considerably in a number of texts that were written between the composition of the Old and New Testaments, and that develop new ideas of a resurrection of the dead and an eternal life with God for the just.

Some of these texts were included in the Greek and Latin versions of the Bible, though they were excluded by non-Hellenistic Jews from the Hebrew Bible. The Christian theologian Jerome called these Apocalyptic texts the 'Apocrypha' (hidden writings, containing esoteric doctrines suitable only for scholars), but most of them are included in the Roman Catholic canon, where they are called 'deutero-canonical books'. Eastern Orthodox Christians, at the Synod of Jerusalem in 1672, excluded most of them from their canon, and many Protestants exclude all of them. Many Protestant Bibles, however, print the Apocrypha between the Old and New Testaments, and parts of them are often read in churches.

This story of the formation of the biblical canon is of great interest theologically, for it shows the need for discrimination in deciding what beliefs are regarded as acceptable in specific churches. Clearly, different Christian churches disagree about the authority to be given to the Apocryphal literature. The Roman Catholic view is the most relaxed, because that church has always held that the magisterium of the church has the sole right to interpret Scripture anyway. So the Church can discriminate between passages that are to be accepted and those that may be ignored or rejected. Many Protestants, for whom the biblical canon is the main rule of faith, exclude the Apocrypha because parts of them conflict with some mainstream Protestant beliefs.

I suggest that arguments about the canonical status of the Apocrypha simply show, in a vivid way, the need for a discriminating interpretation of all Scripture, and the reliance of most believers on some (for them) authoritative interpretation of what is and what is not Scripture. Put bluntly, someone has to decide what texts are to count as a sound basis for faith, and what may be read simply as interesting and important developments in religious thought. In this respect, the Apocrypha certainly show important developments in Jewish thinking about divine justice and life after death, developments without which Jesus' teaching makes much less sense. But, as I have consistently argued, the Bible as a whole should be assessed in the light of our understanding of the love of God as it is disclosed in the person of Jesus. Our final authority is beyond the Bible, though it is expressed to various degrees and in various ways within the Bible.

Within the Apocryphal literature, there is one book of Apocalyptic thought that is of particular importance in showing how beliefs about life after death and divine judgement and mercy were developing from beliefs recorded in earlier biblical documents. This is 2 Esdras, which takes a very forthright view of the divine plan for the human world.

The prophet, supposed to be Ezra, writes that 'The Most High made this world for the sake of many, but the world to come for the sake of only a few ... many have been created, but only a few shall be saved' (2 Esdras 8.1–3). The prophet has the decency to ask if God could not have been more merciful. But he is firmly told by God that 'I will not concern myself about the fashioning of those who have sinned, or about their death, their judgment, or their destruction, but I will rejoice over the creation of the righteous, over their pilgrimage also, and their salvation' (2 Esdras 8.38–39).

These are tough words, and we may be pleased that this book did not make it into the canon. We may also sympathize more with the prophet Ezra than with God (that is, what the prophet believes God said). But it is likely that many early Christians (and many since) have agreed with the more ruthless view. I think it is hardly possible that Jesus would have done.

Jesus called on his disciples not to judge others. So we cannot know whether few or many will be saved (will know and love God for ever). Jesus called for love of enemies, so God would never say, as Ezra's God does, that he does not concern himself with the destruction of millions of human persons. And Jesus taught that God welcomes sinners like the prodigal son, so that God would never declare it impossible for someone to repent.

Ezra is clear that there is judgement on the immorality and injustice of humans, and that there is the possibility of repentance and endless joy with God. He is in fact careful to say that humans will be saved from destruction by their good works, even if they do not know the God of Abraham or obey the Jewish law ('I will give your houses to a people that will come, who without having heard me will believe' (2 Esdras 1.35). Paradise stands waiting for those who 'guard the rights of the widow, secure justice for the ward, give to the needy, defend the orphan, clothe the naked, care for the injured and the weak, do not ridicule the lame, protect the maimed, and let the blind have a vision of my splendour' (2.20–21).

Yet those who do evil will suffer torment in *Gehenna*, and they will be, apparently, the vast majority. Ezra's view is that they have had their chance to follow the way of goodness, and have rejected it. They therefore deserve to suffer, though not for ever. 'They are set on fire and burn hotly, and are extinguished' (7.61). At least their punishment comes to an end.

The prophet is just a little bit too sure that very few will repent, and a little bit too unclear about the limitless patience and love of God. These are things that we may be sure Jesus was clear about, even though some disciples were not. The positive gospel is that God wills all to repent, that repentance is always possible, and that God's love cannot be defeated by evil or death.

This almost certainly means that there is a life beyond physical death in which divine judgement can be expedited, and in which turning to the love of God remains or becomes a real possibility. But in speaking of such a time beyond our physical time human language is strained to the utmost, and there is a danger that symbols will be interpreted as speaking of the near historical future on earth. That is where the interpretation of the symbols of Apocalypse becomes important.

I believe that the clue to unravelling these metaphors of the end of time is to see that they are not about what is to come later in history. We cannot place 'the end of time' in this cosmic space-time at all. That is a major mistake of literalism – to think that the coming of Christ, the trumpet-call, the raising of believers into the clouds, the descent of the New Jerusalem to earth, are literal events that will take place at some time in the future and on the earth.

Talk of the fulfilment of the cosmos is like talk of its creation, in the following way. Creation is not the origin of this space-time, but the total dependence of all spaces and times on one reality beyond them. So the fulfilment of all things in God is not something that happens in the last moments of this space-time, but the taking-up of all spaces and times into the eternal being of God.

Of course, this space-time had a beginning, and it will have an end. There was a first time and there will be a last time. But both of them are relatively boring. The origin is a highly compressed state of infinite mass and density. The end is the emptiness of a cosmos bereft of energy and force, with occasional photons drifting through light-years of nothingness. Almost everything of interest happens in between the beginning and the end. Belief in creation is belief that all those interesting things were envisaged, and the whole system was intended, by God. The purpose of creation is fulfilled when the whole history of the universe is known with full immediacy by God for ever. In that completed divine knowledge all that is imperfect and evil will be sublimated or set aside by full knowledge of its part in the realization of the overwhelmingly good things that the universe generated. All that is good and beautiful will be enjoyed for ever. The Christian hope, founded squarely on the resurrection of Jesus, is that all who respond to God's love will be able to share in that divine knowledge, and realize the purposes of God for lives that were left incomplete on earth.

It is hardly possible for us now to envisage what our lives will then be like. But the Bible has always suggested that human lives are essentially spatial (bodily) and temporal. So we will never exist altogether outside of space and time. We will, however, exist outside this space-time, in a different form of space, without corruption or decay, and in a different form of time, without the forgetfulness (the loss of knowledge of the past) and anxiety (the fear for the future) that mark our present lives. As Paul puts it, 'This perishable body must put on imperishability, and this mortal body must put on immortality' (1 Cor. 15.53).

In a subjective sense, our living in God comes 'after' our earthly time, and is a continuation and consequence of our present experience and actions. Yet there is no physical way of getting from the time of this cosmos to the time of the afterlife. We will be taken into a different form of time, even though we can trace a subjective temporal path from this world to the next. It is like being moved into a parallel universe where, we might say, time flows but the past is never lost, and the future is never insecure.

It is this polar vision of each time being taken into eternity, and yet of eternal life being a continuation and fulfilment of the whole of this life, that the metaphors of 'the end of time' seek to evoke. The relation of each moment of life to eternity is immediate, yet eternal life is the completion of the whole of our earthly lives, and so comes when they are finished.

As it is with each person, so it is with human history as a whole. Each moment of history is directly related to eternity, yet human history is completed in eternity only when it has been completed in this cosmos. If you ask, 'When does eternal life begin?' the answer is 'now', because each present moment is taken into eternity. Yet the answer is also 'at the end of cosmic history', because until every moment of time has been taken into eternity the kingdom will not have come in its fullness. It would be misleading to say that we have to wait billions of years for God's kingdom to come – that would give the impression that it will only exist a very long time from now, and that the present moment is of little relevance to the kingdom. And it would be misleading to say that God's kingdom comes in the immediate future – that would entail that no-one will exist in future to enter it. The paradoxical truth is that each time will be taken into the kingdom, yet all times will have existed and ended before the kingdom comes in its fullness.

The kingdom: a case study

To see the complexity here, let me take a key example, Luke 17.20–37. This is a tremendously obscure passage, and I defy anyone to say that they really know the correct interpretation of it. But I will make some attempt, weak as it is, to see what it could mean.

It starts with a question about when the kingdom of God was coming. This entails that the questioners, the Pharisees, saw the kingdom as future, as coming at some specific time. Jesus' answer sets the tone for all that follows: 'the kingdom of God is not coming with things that can be observed' (verse 20). This seems to be saying that the coming of the kingdom is not a publicly observable event in the future. What is it, then? Jesus says, 'In fact, the kingdom of God is among [or within: *entos*] you.' That means, it is already present, or it is in your hearts.

Many people, including some Pharisees and even the disciples, thought of the kingdom as about to arrive publicly in the near future. But Jesus here says that it is already present in the hearts of those who hear him. This seems to imply that the coming of the kingdom is not a publicly observable event in the future. It is an inward spiritual event in the present. Talk about a future event may lead one to ask unprofitable questions about when exactly it will arrive, whereas talk about a present spiritual possibility puts human lives in question. It asks, 'Will you accept the reality of the kingdom in your life now?' The question then is, what will we do with that inner possibility? Will we accept or reject it in our hearts?

This saying is unique to Luke, but we have to wonder why he places it as the head of this passage, if not to provide the key to interpreting its symbols as speaking of inner present realities, not future public realities. Of course, if the kingdom is an inner reality, it is not fully present, since in the kingdom all will obey God gladly. It exists as an inner anticipation of a future public fulfilment. Luke says there will be no signs for us to tell that the kingdom is near – that rules out all 'reading of the signs', as if we could predict its coming. It is in some sense already present, but as a hidden and ambiguous anticipation of the future. On this reading, Luke does not deny a future fulfilment of the kingdom. But he stresses its present spiritual reality.

Luke immediately moves on to ascribe to the disciples the same misunderstanding that the Pharisees had. They will, says Jesus, long to see 'one of the days of the Son of Man', but they will not do so. The idea seems to be that people might claim that the Son of Man has returned, and is to be found at such and such a place. 'Do not set off in pursuit,' says Jesus. There will be no future public return. If this is correct, then all views that Jesus was a failed prophet of the imminent end of the world are mistaken. He used the language of Apocalyptic thought, but he used it to convey an inward and spiritual message of the dawning of the kingdom in human hearts.

'As the lightning flashes and lights up the sky from one side to the other, so will the Son of Man be (in his day)' (verse 24). If this is a future event, it is one that will be blindingly obvious to all – which suggests that there were those in Luke's day who were inclined to claim that the Son of Man had come in some place or person, not acknowledged by all. Matthew and Mark also allude to such mistaken beliefs. Luke, like them, is certainly denying that possibility. When the Son comes, all will know it. When the kingdom exists in its fullness, evil will have been wholly eradic-ated, and no-one will be in any doubt that the cosmos has been remade.

But if this is at least partly a present inner event, as the first section of this passage asserts, then it suggests that the Son of Man comes like a lightning-flash, illuminating the whole world. Perhaps Luke interpreted this as an inward lightning-flash of illumination. Christ's coming to the heart brings a dramatic and transforming vision of the world and a renewal of life. Luke connects this unambiguously to the person of Jesus by saying that the Son of Man must first suffer and be rejected, before he can come like lightning to human hearts. There is perhaps a double reference to the coming of the risen Christ to human hearts ('it is within you'), and also to the final end of history, which the disciples would not see, but which will ensure that history ends, not with a whimper but with a bang, or at least with a flash.

But now Luke introduces a new theme. In the days of Noah people went about their everyday affairs until the flood came and destroyed them all. They ignored God's warnings, and persisted in the evil of their hearts, unaware of the destruction that would engulf them. We are not thinking here of millions of ordinary people who are doing their best to do what is right. We are thinking of a people of whom it is said that 'every inclination of the thoughts of their hearts was only evil continually' (Gen. 6.5). It is those who are wholly committed to absolute evil who will suddenly be destroyed – but remember that this is not to be a public future event. It is inward and present. So the destruction is the spiritual death of those who are wholly and irrevocably committed to evil.

In the days of Lot, too, Luke says, the outcry against the people of Sodom had become great before the Lord (Gen. 19.13). Those people were devoted to wickedness for its own sake, and they were destroyed by fire. Wickedness brings judgement and destruction, that much is clear. But what is meant by saying that 'it will be like that on the day that the Son of Man is revealed' (Luke 17.30)? When will these things be? They are present within you, says Jesus. When the Son of Man is revealed, in the divine encounter with the person of Jesus, it will mean the destruction of all evil.

Insofar as this passage refers to the end of history, the implication is that evil will be utterly destroyed. But then Luke inserts a passage which does not seem to make much sense. He says that a man on a house roof should not come down to collect his possessions. Where is the man supposed to be going? In Matthew and Mark, this saying belongs with warnings that Jerusalem will be destroyed, and that people should flee without waiting to pick up their belongings. There it makes good sense. Luke, however, has placed the saying in the context of the destruction of the world, and there is nowhere to flee! Why has he done so? The clue comes in the saying, 'Remember Lot's wife' (verse 32), with the associated saying, also in Matthew and John in slightly differing forms: 'Those who try to make their life secure will lose it' (verse 33).

Do not try to keep your belongings safe; do not try to make sure that your home is secure. In other words, do not remain entangled with worldly affairs and fears. This appears to be the spiritual teaching of this passage. In John it is clearest: 'He who hates his life in this world will keep it for eternal life' (John 12.25). Do not aim at security in the world, but be prepared to give up all for Christ. That is the only way of escaping judgement.

The stories of Noah and Lot are thus used as metaphors for a general statement that allying yourself with 'the world' (the structures of greed and hatred) brings destruction. But being unconcerned with possessions, and seeking to 'die with Christ', will gain eternal life. The use of the otherwise senseless statement about not going down to collect your possessions makes sense when it is seen, not as a statement about the future, but as a symbolic way of speaking about human attachment to possessions, and the importance of renouncing the world.

It is not that if, one day in the near future, you see lightning flash across the sky, you should build an ark or flee from Sodom. It is not even clear what you should do, exactly. It is rather that, if Christ appears to you like a lightning-flash, this will be life and not destruction only if you put aside all worldly concerns for security and give your life wholly to Christ.

The passage concludes with the comment, also found in Matthew, 'On that night there will be two in one bed; one will be taken and the other left' (verse 34). Those who suppose that this refers to an actual physical 'rapture', with people disappearing from their beds in the night, leaving very worried partners behind, have ignored the opening statement of this passage that Jesus is not speaking of public events. They also have no way of accounting for the fact that if everything has already been destroyed, there will be nobody left to be 'taken'. The best way to make sense of Luke's putting first the destruction of a wholly evil world, then the warning against 'looking back', and finally the 'rapture', is to say that they all refer to the spiritual necessity of leaving the world of corruption and death, and living in Christ. The 'taking' and the 'leaving' are inner events. Those left are left to spiritual destruction, and those taken are saved from it.

It is a natural question that the disciples ask: 'Where, Lord?' Where are people taken? Jesus' answer is again cryptic and allusive: 'Where the corpse is, there the vultures will gather' (verse 37). I do not think anyone takes this literally, as if they are taken to visit a corpse with some vultures. Perhaps, as vultures fly to a dead body, so they will be taken to where the living body of the risen and glorified Christ is, to Paradise and the presence of God, to live with him for ever.

This is a difficult passage. But if the clue to its interpretation is given in its first section, then these are metaphors used primarily to convey an inward and spiritual meaning. Christ (the Son of Man) pierces the outer facades of human beings and exposes their inmost secrets like a lightning-flash, illumining their lives either as committed to hatred, oppression and depravity, which lead to destruction, or as prepared to give up their lives, turn to Christ, and be taken to live with Christ, being liberated by him from hatred, greed and ignorance.

This may seem not much like a positive gospel, after all. For it seems that most people will indeed be judged and found wanting – 'many are called, but few are chosen' (Matt. 22.14). We need to bear in mind that Jesus is positively calling people to life, not condemning them to death. It is just a statement of fact that most people will not genuinely respond to his call to die to self and live for God alone. In that sense they will be spiritually dead, and fall under judgement. Serious though this is, a gospel of unlimited divine love will never assert that those people are condemned for ever without hope of reprieve. We may be sure that God will never give up on them, but will continue to reach out to them in this life and in whatever life comes after this. God does not say, 'This is your one and only chance, after which you are doomed.' God says, 'See the suffering and spiritual death to which your present life is leading. Accept life and joy instead. I will make it possible for you.' Then, hopefully, you will be part of the vanguard of the whole human world as it finally returns to God.

When is the kingdom of God coming? It comes as Christ encounters us, reveals our most inward and hidden condition, and calls us to turn from the world towards eternal life. That happened as Jesus physically encountered those he met in Galilee and Jerusalem ('The kingdom is among you'). It happens to people throughout the world as the risen Christ encounters millions of people in the secret places of their hearts ('The kingdom is within you'). Christ is the lightning-bolt that exposes what we are, that calls us to die to self and follow him, liberated from the world of selfishness and destruction into the open sky of love and joy. That is liberation into the kingdom of God, and that is how and when the kingdom comes.

I think this is what Luke is trying to convey, but it does not mean that the 'coming of the Son of Man', or of the kingdom of God, is a purely subjective matter of turning from evil to good. The destruction of evil is real. Eternal life is real. The risen and glorified Christ is real. One day, probably only at the end of human history, all evil will be eliminated. Those who live with Christ do have real continuing lives which extend beyond bodily death. Christ will be fully known and present to all who turn to him – that is the *Par-ousia*, the 'being-present', of the return in glory, of Christ. The end of history will not be a dissolution into nothingness. It will be the final victory of goodness, and of all the good that this cosmos has generated in its long struggle to realize communities of love and freedom from the dust of dying stars.

These are the fundamentals of Christian faith in the future. Luke presents them in a series of vivid images. But he does so in a way that emphasizes the importance of the presence of Christ within, and the kingdom of God as a dynamic reality taking shape in the lives of men and women of every generation. When is the kingdom coming? When the Son of Man comes to us like a flash of lightning, revealing the self-destructive nature of evil, calling us to follow him without looking back to the desires of the world that once bound us, raising us to live with him in the presence of God. And in this present inward encounter with the eternal Christ, we dimly foresee and to some extent anticipate and make present the ultimate future that God intends, of a society of free, loving and creative persons, sharers in the nature of God, participants in the life of eternity.

It is perhaps important to say that *one should not attempt to decode these symbols in a detailed way*, as if each element of the metaphor signified something precise. Thus when Jesus says we shall 'eat with Abraham . . . in the kingdom of heaven' (Matt. 8.11), it is vain to ask what the menu will be, what Abraham will be wearing or how many courses there are. The image makes the point that all those who have died will share together in the life of God. The Abrahamic feast is a symbol for a universal spiritual communion, and it would miss the point to suppose that there will be an actual table and actual food.

Similarly, when Jesus says that he will raise the dead on the Last Day (John 6.40), that does not really mean that there will be an actual day on which all the dead will climb from their tombs. The point is that those who have died will be accountable for their lives, but will also be confronted by the offer of God's redeeming grace. This does not happen on one specific day, or in this physical cosmos at all. But there is a claim that there will be judgement and grace beyond physical death.

The Gospels use such symbols of the prophetic tradition to interpret the destruction of Jerusalem and the birth and spread of the Church despite persecution – seen as anticipations of the attainment of God's final goal. Jesus, whom they believed to be not only a prophet, but also the Messianic redeeming King of Israel, was made central to a radical re-formulation of the prophetic symbols, according to which the 'elect remnant' was to be no longer a nation, but a universal communion called out of all nations. Jesus, the teacher of the kingdom that had drawn near, was the one who was believed to have died to offer his life as an atoning sacrifice uniting the kingdoms of heaven and earth. He was the one they believed to have risen from death, and he was seen as the king who rules in the kingdom of the Spirit. His rule remains real though hidden until the final fulfilment of God's purpose.

Did Jesus think of himself thus? Historians have no way of telling. We can only say that early Christians thought this of Jesus. But we can say that such thoughts would not have been impossible for a Jewish prophet of great spiritual stature with a strong sense of vocation. Though the disciples could have been deluded, the commitment even to death of those who had known Jesus and witnessed to his resurrection is strong testimony to their reliability and veracity. If we are inclined to accept a spiritual basis of reality, and the general authenticity of Hebrew prophetic insights into the moral and providential character of God, then we may reasonably see Jesus as what he was claimed to be, the fulfilment of the prophetic tradition. Add to this an acceptance of the Church as the medium of life-transforming discernments of God, and as the carrier of a developing tradition of spiritual understanding, and we have a strong basis for a commitment of faith that Jesus was and knew himself to be what the disciples claimed him to be, the liberator of humanity from sin and the king of a renewed Israel.

Did they believe that Jesus would return soon, bringing in God's final goal? Some of them certainly did, though they were warned that, while they should live as if he might return at any moment, they should beware of looking for specific signs or believing alleged reports of that return. Given the world-view of the time, it was reasonable to think that history might end soon with the coming of God's kingdom, and Jesus may have thought that too. But such Apocalyptic passages form a very small part of the New Testament writings, and are qualified by a sense that the gospel should be spread throughout the whole world before the End. The important spiritual belief is that God's kingdom will come, evil will be eliminated, and Jesus seen by all as the unifier of humanity and divinity. That remains the basic Christian hope for the cosmos. If we see it as fulfilled beyond this space-time realm altogether, then the historical timing does not matter – though it still makes sense to live and act as if the End was near to us, embracing every present and transfiguring it by its inclusion in the life of eternity.

Part 5

THE DEVELOPMENT OF IDEAS IN THE BIBLE

The development of biblical ideas of God and morality

<hr/>

In Part 4 I have described the way in which scholarly study of the New Testament leads to a recognition of development in biblical ideas of the kingdom of God and of the ultimate destiny of human beings. Jesus used the ideas of Apocalyptic literature in his teaching of the kingdom, but he developed them in a new way. Study of the New Testament documents suggests that Jesus' teaching was sometimes understood in a restrictive and judgemental way by his disciples. Further developments of understanding are required if we are to embrace the whole range of New Testament writings, and allow our understanding to be guided by what I have held are the key teachings of Jesus about forgiveness, unlimited love, and the kingdom as a primarily spiritual reality.

Biblical scholarship can help us to achieve a clearer view of the metaphorical nature of much biblical language, and to see how there are lines of development in the Bible that may yet be pursued further. In this final part I will specifically address the question of the development of biblical ideas, and show how the idea of such development is essential to a proper understanding of the Bible in the light of modern scholarship.

The Bible is the oldest written record we have of the gradual development of ideas of God within one continuous religious tradition. It seems very likely that the earliest forms of human religion posited a number of local gods and spirits, with one local god being specially associated with a particular tribe. There are traces of such a view in the Bible, for which the God of Abraham is one of many gods. Psalm 95 says, 'The LORD is a great God, and a great King above all gods' (verse 3). Certainly the God of Israel is the greatest of the gods, but other nations have their gods too. 'Is there another nation on earth whose God went to redeem it as a people ... by driving out before his people nations and their gods?' (2 Sam. 7.23). Each nation has its own god, but the God of Israel is greater. 'The LORD is greater than all gods, because he delivered the people from the Egyptians' (Exod. 18.11). 'Our God is greater than other gods' (2 Chron. 2.5).

Though such a belief in many gods is found in the Bible, it soon developed into the belief that Israel's God is in fact the only god. So 1 Chronicles 16.25–26 says, 'Great is the LORD ... he is to be revered above all gods. For all the gods of the peoples are idols, but the LORD made the heavens.' The God of Israel is not just the greatest god. He is the creator of all things, and so the other 'gods' do not really exist, or are at best inadequate representations of the one true God. This process is completed by the time of the major prophets. 'I am the first and I am the last; besides me there is no god' (Isa. 44.6). From belief that there is no god to be compared with Israel's God Isaiah definitively moves to affirm that there is actually no god that actually exists apart from the God of Abraham. All other 'gods' are empty images, with no reality at all. When the Genesis creation story was written, quite late in Israel's history, it is made quite clear that one God created all things.

The Bible shows the development of monotheism in Israel. It also shows a development in the idea of God's goodness. Some early stories exemplify a belief in God's power as a dangerous energy that can break out and destroy those who come too close. Such a belief is characteristic of many tribal and pre-literate societies, where taboos guard the breaking-out of holy and destructive power. When David first tried to bring the Ark of the Covenant to Jerusalem, an unfortunate character called Uzzah put out his hand to steady the Ark, and 'the anger of the LORD was kindled against Uzzah; he struck him down' (1 Chron. 13.10). Here God is depicted as angry because someone dares to touch a sacred object without being properly sanctified. In the historical perspective of the history of religions, this is quite a common belief. Sacred objects, which embody or communicate the presence of God, carry a dangerous power, and only certain persons, using special rituals, may touch them. The Exodus account of Moses' ascent of Mount Sinai carries a similar thought: 'The LORD said to Moses, "Go down and warn the people not to break through to the LORD to look; otherwise many of them will perish"' (Exod. 19.21).

Taken out of historical context, this seems like a superstitious belief in the danger of sacred power, which needs to be handled with care and surrounded with protective rituals. To understand it we have to know something about the beliefs of tribal societies, and the ways in which they regard the sacred powers surrounding them as powerful energies that need to be contained, isolated or placated.

Looking back at these stories and rituals from a Christian point of view, we can say that they do convey a true sense of the awesome power of God, and the necessity of reverence before the ultimate power of Being. But it is a very partial view of God – not yet aware of the nature of God as unlimited love and grace, and too much wedded to the efficacy of rituals and animal sacrifices to placate God, instead of the true obedience of the heart that the prophets were later to see much more clearly.

The prophet Amos was to see it: 'I hate, I despise your festivals . . . the offerings of well-being of your fatted animals I will not look upon . . . but let justice roll down like waters, and righteousness like an ever-flowing stream' (Amos 5.21–24). In reading the Bible, it is important to see this development of understanding from a reliance on rituals and sacrifices to placate an angry God to the realization that love of God and neighbour is the religion that God requires. Not to see that development, but to take every part of the Bible as equally accurate and adequate in its descriptions of God, is to misinterpret the message of Scripture in a fundamental way.

Nevertheless, the early passages cannot be simply ignored (though many Christians have wanted to do so, setting aside the Old Testament entirely). There is something about God that these ancient writings show, however one-sidedly. God is not just a kindly old man in the sky. God is the ultimate power of the cosmos, truly awe-inspiring, terrifying and vast almost beyond imagination. We should approach God with fear and trembling, with reverence and respect. Because our hearts are turned away from God and towards selfish desire, we should fear the judgement of God. Even though, as Christians, we believe that God on the cross has paid the penalty that divine judgement requires, we can never take it for granted. We may feel we have passed beyond the need for ritual sacrifice and a belief that God may destroy us for some mistake in the ritual – and we have. Yet we must come before God with a sense of awe, and in awareness that the one true sacrifice of the cross is the only path to knowledge and love of God.

For Christians the whole religious structure of animal sacrifice has been set aside. An important part of the law of God, the Torah, which the Bible says was given to Moses, is concerned with the rules for animal sacrifice. All Christians believe that such sacrifices have been rendered unnecessary, because they have been fulfilled in the self-sacrifice of Jesus on the cross. It follows that Christians must accept a development in human knowledge of God. If God no longer requires sacrifice, then the sacrificial system must have been a temporary and relatively incomplete way of relating truly to God. As Christian theologians have usually said, the Temple sacrifices point forward to, they anticipate in a way that was not fully perceived, something they did not envisage: the sacrifice of the cross.

Paul said that the law was a schoolmaster, a 'disciplinarian': 'the law was our disciplinarian until Christ came' (Gal. 3.24). Now that Christ has come, we are no longer subject to such discipline. The law contains something authentic in our knowledge of God. But it is surpassed, for Christians, by the New Testament, with its message of new life in the Spirit. For this reason, Christians are committed to believing that there is a development of insight in the Bible. The first five books of the Bible clearly lay down a ritual and moral system of laws. But the letters of the New Testament state that Christians do not have to obey those laws.

Paul struggled with the problem of whether Christians should just ditch the Hebrew Bible altogether, in his letter to the Romans. His final recommendation was that we should retain the Hebrew Bible, for, as the writer of Timothy says, 'all scripture is inspired by God' (2 Tim. 3.16) – where by 'scripture' the writer meant the Hebrew Bible. But of course the writer did not mean that we should carry out the sacrifices prescribed in Leviticus. He meant that the Hebrew Bible, taken as a whole, could be seen as pointing to Christ as the fulfilment of prophecy.

That is something, however, that the Hebrew Bible itself did not know, and does not say. Almost all Jews who take the Hebrew Bible as their Scripture deny that it says any such thing. What Christians have to do is to re-interpret the Hebrew Bible in such a way that it can be seen as pointing to Jesus as the Messiah. In other words, Christians have to project their belief in Jesus back onto the ancient texts, and interpret the texts in the light of later developments that are not in the texts themselves. That is what development means. The Old Testament shows a growing belief that there is one creator God whose nature is universal redeeming love, and who will be revealed as a suffering servant of all (Isa. 52 and 53), not as the vengeful destroyer of all the earth.

New Testament developments
of biblical ideas

In being Christians, we inherit this developing tradition. It is important not to deny that it is our tradition. It is equally important to see that it develops over many centuries, and to note that not all developments are positive. Some of the later passages (for example, when Nehemiah beat and pulled out the hair of Israelites who had married foreign women; Neh. 13.25) are less tolerant and more vindictive than some key passages in Isaiah.

We can say, with the New Testament writer, that 'no prophecy of scripture is a matter of one's own interpretation . . . but men and women moved by the Holy Spirit spoke from God' (2 Pet. 1.20–21). The Spirit has moved in the hearts and minds of these prophets so that what they write continues a developing tradition that will culminate in the birth of Jesus. But the Spirit does not remove all the prejudices and peculiarities of their characters and temperaments. In order to discern what is lasting and true in their writings, we need to see Jesus as the one to whom they point, and who corrects, fulfils and amplifies their more limited, but still God-inspired, vision.

Ideas of God develop in the Bible from belief in one 'Lord of Armies' (the 'LORD of Hosts', 1 Sam. 4.4) who is often angry and visits the sins of the fathers on their children to the third generation, to Jesus' teaching of a loving Father who will go to any lengths to save those who are lost in sin, and whose forgiveness is without limit.

Throughout the Bible, God is conceived as one who cares for Israel, has liberated the Hebrew tribes from slavery and makes a covenant with them for ever. But we can see how in the early stages Jahweh was thought of as basically a tribal god, unconcerned with the rest of the world, and felt more as a fearsome power than as a loving Father. The prophetic vision of God developed gradually, as mercy, goodness and love were seen as more appropriate to God than sheer overwhelming power and glory. God's concern was with the whole world, not just with Israel, and the covenant was a calling to service, not to military triumph. These things, for Christians, become clear in the teaching of Jesus, whose life, as the perfect Jew, was one of service, love and forgiveness, and who rejected the exclusivism of those Pharisees who put obedience to the letter of the law above human compassion.

Jesus also criticized some rather moralistic trends in early Hebrew monotheism. Some parts of the Bible take an over-simple view of God's reactions to good and evil. 'I have been young, and now am old, yet I have not seen the righteous forsaken or their children begging bread' (Ps. 37.25). God rewards the righteous with many children and cattle, but he punishes the wicked with destruction. There are thoughts here of immediate rewards and punishments for good and bad conduct. But they are thoughts which many biblical passages treat with total scepticism. The book of Job is one long rejection of the view that those who flourish are good and those who suffer must have done evil.

Jesus said, '[God] makes his sun rise on the evil and on the good, and sends rain on the righteous and on the unrighteous' (Matt. 5.45). There is no direct correlation between earthly success and goodness, and the evil often prosper. Jesus himself was killed as a criminal, though he was innocent of any crime. So there is no biblical justification for the view that the innocent will escape disaster. Rather, the Bible contains a mixture of different views, some of them naively thinking that God directly acts to reward good and punish evil, but others, like Job, finding that even evil comes ultimately from God, and falls on innocent and guilty alike.

The Bible definitely affirms that God acts. God acted to liberate Israel, and acts in Jesus to redeem the world. But those acts do not always come in the way we expect or desire. The 'co-operative action' that I am suggesting as the mode of God's activity in the world is a real causal influence in the world. But it co-operates with the necessities of the fundamental laws and structures of creation and with the free acts of finite persons. So God's particular acts of judgement and grace, which are real and effective, are nevertheless interwoven with many complex currents of the necessities of nature and the contingencies of history. Israel was liberated from Egypt – but then wandered for forty years in the wilderness. Jesus' disciples saw the kingdom of God – but many of them were tortured and killed for their loyalty to Christ.

God has a moral goal which is to be achieved by the co-operative actions of human beings. But even for the great prophets this goal tends to be depicted in terms of an earthly future of glory for Israel. All the scattered tribes will return to Jerusalem, and all nations shall come to worship in the Temple. The hope of a time of peace and fulfilment – *shalom* – is for all the world: 'my house shall be called a house of prayer for all peoples' (Isa. 56.7). Yet Israel will be the greatest nation: 'nations that do not know you shall run to you . . . for [God] has glorified you' (Isa. 55.5). Nationalism has not quite been overcome, even in this universal vision of peace. And, of course, the hope is that in this new age the Torah will be fully kept in all its details.

Christians do not usually accept the hope quite in this form, though they take it as a pointer to what they do accept – the dawning of the kingdom of God. Christians do not expect the restoration of sacrifices in the Temple in Jerusalem, or the universal re-institution of Jewish law. Most crucially, Christians think the Messiah has already come, in the person of Jesus, and now reigns 'at the right hand of God', in power.

In order for this belief to be maintained, Christians have to revise the idea of the Messiah quite radically, even though they may justly claim that their revision is hinted at by many parts of the Hebrew Bible. Jesus as Messiah did not overthrow Roman military power and establish a new Temple in Jerusalem, to which all people will travel to worship. Jesus died as a common criminal, and his resurrection and Ascension were hidden from the public gaze. His kingdom is 'not from this world' (John 18.36). It is not an earthly kingdom, and he enters into glory as he enters into Paradise. When the penitent thief says, 'Remember me when you come into your kingdom,' Jesus replies, 'Today you will be with me in Paradise' (Luke 23.42 and 43). Jesus comes into his kingdom in Paradise, not in the earthly Jerusalem some time in the historical future. Jerusalem is the heavenly city, and the Temple is the body of Christ, the existence of the redeemed in the presence of God.

One main reason Christians cannot take all the Bible as literally true and inerrant is that they have to re-interpret most of it completely in a way that Jews (surely the best interpreters of the Hebrew Bible – that is, the vast majority of the Bible) would not accept, and in the light of the new revelation of God in the person of Jesus. That new revelation forces Christians to accept a radical development of most biblical (Old Testament) ideas, and to give many of them a spiritual interpretation.

To give Jerusalem and the Temple a spiritual interpretation is not to say that they are not real or objective. It is to say that they refer to a non-earthly, non-material reality – basically, to the objective reality of God, and to the community of all those who are related to God in reverence, thankfulness and love.

Is there such a non-material reality? God is certainly such a reality. Though the Bible often refers to God as having a body – God walks in the Garden of Eden, and sits on a throne – these are metaphors for a God who has no earthly form: 'To whom will you liken me and make me equal, and compare me, as though we were alike?' (Isa. 46.5). Images of God are prohibited in Hebrew thought precisely because God is not like anything finite. The reality of God is beyond space and time, and beyond every finite physical form.

This is true even of Jesus. Even though Christians have mostly decided that it is permissible to depict Jesus pictorially, and to say that Jesus is the incarnation of God, nevertheless the divinity of Jesus cannot be portrayed, and it would be quite wrong to say that God just is the physical Jesus. Jesus truly presents an image of God in human form; but the reality of the Word of God that is truly expressed in Jesus is far beyond any human form. 'God is spirit' (John 4.24) – consciousness, wisdom and perfect beauty. Paradise, where Jesus and the penitent thief were to meet, is no earthly or material place. Paradise is a realm beyond this space-time where finite spirits form a community which can have true knowledge of God, the Supreme Spirit.

The development of biblical ideas of the afterlife

To speak of a spiritual realm is to speak of a life beyond this earthly life. Christians are committed to such a belief. Jesus rose from death, and does not now live somewhere in outer space. He lives in the spiritual realm, where we also hope to live when this life is ended: 'if for this life only we have hoped in Christ, we are of all people most to be pitied' (1 Cor. 15.19).

The idea of life after death was slow to develop in the Bible. The Hebrews did not look forward to a life after death. The world of the dead, *Sheol*, is described in the book of Job as 'the land of gloom and deep darkness, the land of gloom and chaos, where light is like darkness' (Job 10.21–22). There the dead have some sort of semi-existence, as shadows of the beings they were. King Saul consulted a medium from Endor, and she called up the spirit of Samuel, who said, 'Why have you disturbed me by bringing me up?' (1 Sam. 28.15). The dead in some sense still exist. But it is hardly a pleasant existence. 'In death there is no remembrance of you; in Sheol who can give you praise?' (Ps. 6.5).

This is not the sort of Paradise in which Jesus and the thief meet after death. It is only in the later Old Testament that a more positive belief in life after death is found, in the idea of a resurrection of the dead. 'Many of those who sleep in the dust of the earth shall awake,' says the book of Daniel (Dan. 12.2). Yet that hope for resurrection was not universally accepted. In the time of Jesus, the Sadducees, a traditionalist movement, refused to accept the resurrection of the dead, and their view was perfectly orthodox.

Jesus, along with the Pharisees, certainly did teach the reality of a resurrection from death. But his view was a definite development from the vague and tentative Old Testament hopes. Belief in the

132

resurrection of the dead probably arose in later Jewish reflection (between the Old and New Testaments) on the martyrdom of the Maccabean revolutionaries, who, it came to be thought by many Jews, must have their reward from God.

There were many differing beliefs at the time of Jesus about just what the resurrection of the dead might be. There were some rather materialistic views that the dead would climb from their tombs at some time in the future, and live on a renewed earth. Matthew's account of the resurrection of Jesus says that 'many bodies of the saints who had fallen asleep were raised . . . they came out of the tombs and entered the holy city' (Matt. 27.52–53). That is a very materialist account of resurrection, and it is consistent with Matthew's highly embroidered narrative of a great earthquake, the tearing of the Temple curtain, and three hours of darkness at the moment of crucifixion.

One reason for seeing Matthew's narrative as highly embroidered is that most of the other accounts of Jesus' resurrection are not materialist at all. The body of Jesus could appear suddenly in a locked room, disappear just as suddenly, and be unrecognized on a seven-mile walk to Emmaus until the 'breaking of bread' (Luke 24.30–31). After a time, his body ceased to appear on earth at all in physical form. So it seems that Jesus appeared in a fully bodily form (speaking, moving, eating bread and fish, for instance), but that the true form of his resurrection body was not physical in any ordinary sense.

Paul confirms this in his account of seeing the risen Christ. He did not see a human body, but a dazzling and blinding light (Acts 9.3). When Paul comes to write about the resurrection bodies we will all have, he is clear that 'flesh and blood cannot inherit the kingdom of God' (1 Cor. 15.50), but that 'this perishable body must put on imperishability' (verse 53). We will have new, imperishable, immortal and 'spiritual' bodies.

The idea seems to be that we will exist in some form of embodiment, where social relationships and activities are possible, but it will be quite different from earthly embodiment. The resurrection world, the 'new creation', the full and final realization of the kingdom of God, will not be in the future of this space-time.

The goal of this cosmos lies beyond this cosmos, in a form of being which is the consequence of what happens in this cosmos, and which could not have existed without this cosmos, because it is the realm of beings who were born and lived first in this cosmos. Paul's analogy is unequivocal: 'You do not sow the body that is to be, but a bare seed' (1 Cor. 15.37). Our earthly physical bodies are the seeds from which our spiritual bodies will grow. What we shall become is the result of what we have made of what we now are. 'What we will be has not yet been revealed. What we do know is this: when he is revealed, we will be like him, for we will see him as he is' (1 John 3.2).

This idea of the spiritual kingdom as the goal of history is a radically new idea that results from the disciples' experience of the risen Jesus. It is a major development from all Old Testament speculations about the afterlife, and a re-location of our ultimate hope from this world to the world beyond, a spiritual world that shares the life of God. This is such a transformation of biblical (Old Testament) hopes that it may seem the Old Testament can simply be ignored, and that we should start again with Christ. That has been a persistent Christian temptation throughout history. But what the Old Testament shows, for Christians, is Christ as the fulfilment of biblical hopes, not just as their negation ('I have come not to abolish but to fulfil', Matt. 5.17). Christians must see the biblical record as a long history of developing insights into the nature and purposes of God, with the vision of Christ in glory as the key to interpreting that historical record and the test by which all its particular texts must be judged.

We should not be too confident of our speculations about the afterlife. It is spoken of in metaphors and images, seeking to convey in different ways the reality of Jesus' appearances in glory to his disciples, the reality of our hope in Christ that we shall be like him, and a hope that all human beings without exception will come finally to the vision of Christ in glory, and be offered eternal companionship with God through him.

Much of Jesus' teaching seems to imply that the dead think and speak before the general resurrection. In his parable of the rich man and Lazarus (Luke 16.19–31), Lazarus is carried to Abraham's bosom, while the rich man suffers torment in Hades (*Sheol*). This implies some form of conscious life, either pleasant or unpleasant, before a final Judgement Day.

Jesus said that God is 'God not of the dead, but of the living' (Luke 20.38), which implies that Abraham and Isaac were in some sense alive at the time he said this. Jesus was seen by Peter, James and John in a vision, speaking with Moses and Elijah (Luke 9.28–36). The strange story in 1 Peter (1 Pet. 3.18–22, and 4.6) about Jesus descending to the world of the dead and preaching to them entails that the dead can hear and respond before the day of resurrection. And if, as seems likely, Jesus ascended to glory after his resurrection – 'There are some standing here who will not taste death before they see the Son of Man coming in his kingdom' (Matt. 16.28) – then he began his rule in the kingdom at the Ascension. This suggests that the kingdom of God exists in heaven, in Paradise, and that there Christ rules with the saints in glory.

Yet the New Testament does speak of a 'day of resurrection', when all the dead will rise and hear the voice of Christ, and of a Judgement Day before the throne of God. And it does say that the dead 'sleep' in Christ, which implies that they are not conscious.

What then are we to say? It seems to me that the strongest and most reliable claim is the testimony of the disciples that they had seen Jesus risen, a claim that changed their lives for ever. He at least was fully alive, and enthroned at God's right hand, after his physical death. Is it likely that he was the only human person to be alive? The recorded vision of him speaking with Moses and Elijah could be a literary invention to make the point that he fulfilled the law and the prophets. But if we think it was a genuine vision, then at least some other human figures live 'in heaven' (Elijah was taken up to heaven in a chariot, Enoch was widely believed to have been taken up to heaven – Genesis 5.24 – and Moses was said in Jewish tradition to have been assumed into heaven). There is a heaven, a Paradise, and the saints live in it, even before the resurrection. Christ assumes lordship over the kingdom of heaven at his Ascension.

Not all humans enter the kingdom. 'Many are called, but few are chosen' (Matt. 22.14). Indeed, it may seem that very few indeed are prepared to be full members of a kingdom of selfless love.

We are all called to that destiny, but few indeed are those who manage to respond adequately. And the hard question is: what of those who are not chosen? No doubt they have failed to love and to respond to God as they ought. No doubt they deserve some sort of penalty for the harm they have caused and the wrong they have done. Prison might be an appropriate metaphor for what they deserve to endure. But will that state continue for ever, without any hope of remission?

Such a thought seems impossible to square with the unlimited love of God that is revealed in Jesus. And that, I think, is the ultimate test. Jesus' resurrection shows that there is a life beyond death. Jesus' crucifixion shows that God will go to any lengths to seek and to save those who are lost in sin. Jesus' teaching shows that we should be like God in practising unlimited forgiveness and mercy, loving even our enemies and wishing their good (Matt. 5.44–45). In the light of these facts, what are we to think of God's attitude to those who are lost in selfish desire, unable to love others with their whole hearts, and blind to the presence of God?

I have argued, especially in Part 4, that God's attitude will be one of unceasing and unchangeable concern for the well-being of all his creatures. As 1 Timothy 2.3–4 says: 'God our Saviour . . . desires everyone to be saved and to come to the knowledge of the truth.' If men and women turn from God, if they destroy the world God has created, and torture and kill other human beings, of course God cannot just say, 'I don't mind; come to heaven anyway.' There is a price to be paid for evil. But God still desires the salvation of all who must pay that price; that is a basic Christian truth.

It is for that reason that the Church, while insisting that there is a hell, a state of regret, remorse, anger and hatred to which loveless lives condemn themselves, has also introduced the idea of Purgatory, a state where sin can be purged and minds returned to the love which is their proper calling. But the Church has had a very limited and exclusive view of who gets to go to Purgatory. Traditionally you have to die in a state of grace, which has sometimes been very narrowly interpreted as dying as a baptized Christian.

That undermines the unlimited nature of the divine love. In recent years, some emphasis has been placed upon the concepts of 'implicit desire' and 'invincible ignorance' to make the traditional view rather less narrow. Then we can say that people may die with implicit desires to be Christians, if only they had not been invincibly ignorant, and so failed to see what Christ really is and what the love of God really is. That is a great moral improvement on the belief that all who do not explicitly accept Christ are condemned.

But why not widen the gate a little further, and say that even those who had no implicit desires to be Christians, and who had chosen against God in their earthly lives, might yet repent and believe, after further experience of where such attitudes lead them? That is what 1 Peter 3.20 and 4.6 seem to say. The gospel is proclaimed even to the dead who had not obeyed God during their lives, who had been drowned in the great flood for their wickedness. Even then, one cannot guarantee that they will live in the Spirit. But at least they will have had a real opportunity. The door of repentance has not been closed by the rather arbitrary fact of earthly death. It will only be closed when and if their decision is irrevocable. And no-one on earth can say when that might be.

If we look at Jesus' parables about judgement, we can see that they do envisage a great divide between being thrown on the fire (*Gehenna*, the fire outside Jerusalem on which rubbish is burned, is the word translated as 'hell' in many Bibles) and being 'gathered into a barn' (Matt. 13.30), or between age-long (*aionios*) life and age-long punishment. There is judgement, and it is serious. On the other hand, Jesus' whole life is a demonstration of the mercy and self-giving love of God. Jesus came not to judge, but to give life (John 3.17). It would be a travesty of such love to say that life will only be given to those who have heard of and follow Jesus as Lord. We cannot state the conditions under which God may give life to someone, except to say that there must be an inward assent to God in the heart, though God may not be explicitly recognized as such. God comes to give life, but we may still choose darkness (John 3.19). God's offer of life will remain open without limit, even when God's judgement on evil is taking effect.

This is a prime example of the way in which the search for a biblical view on afterlife requires sensitive discrimination, and the discernment of those texts which carry the decisive elements of

Christian teaching against which other texts may be judged. Some may take the texts about eternal punishment as decisive, and then interpret texts like 'God has imprisoned all in disobedience so that he may be merciful to all' (Rom. 11.32), and 'God . . . the saviour of all people' (1 Tim. 4.10), as exaggerated and literally false. Others, like me, will take texts about God's unlimited forgiveness and God's desire that all should be saved (1 Tim. 2.3) as decisive, and then interpret the judgement texts as metaphorical statements outlining possibilities of destruction which we may hope and pray will never be actually realized for anyone.

How can we decide? Not from the texts themselves. Choices have to be made. And our choices must be illuminated by our beliefs about the person of Jesus, about whether he himself is primarily stern and judgemental or universally compassionate and forgiving. It is because of this that, while Scripture is the book that shows us Christ, Christ is the person who must govern our interpretation of Scripture.

I have given my views on the afterlife more fully in *What the Bible Really Teaches*, chapter 9, so I will not repeat them here. But at the time of Jesus those who believed in an afterlife did not think of the torments of 'the prison' as lasting for ever. The penalty of sin could be paid, and then release was possible. It is overwhelmingly likely, then, that Jesus' view of *Sheol* did not imply that any torments to be endured would be literally without end.

A case study in development:
retributive and restorative justice

The crucial issue is what sort of punishment for evil we would think to be appropriate for an unlimitedly loving God. A purely retributive theory would hold that there is a set punishment for a crime and it must be paid, whatever the consequences for the criminal and for the victims, whether those consequences are good or bad.

Pure retributivism is a backward-looking theory. You do not take future consequences of punishment into account, but simply look back at the gravity of the crime, and insist that the due penalty be paid. For some Christians, any sin against God is of infinite gravity, and so the penalty will be infinite, or endless. So the doctrine of endless torment in hell arose. But it depends on thinking that every sin against God is of infinite gravity, which may seem disproportionate, especially if the sinners do not even believe in God. And it depends on denying the possibility of a change of heart after death, which seems to limit the scope of God's redeeming love in an unacceptable way.

A different view of justice is what came to be called 'restorative justice' in South Africa after the ending of apartheid. There is an element of retribution, for the offender must truly feel the gravity of his or her offence, and must suffer a deprivation of good because of the offence. Yet restorative justice also takes into account the consequences of punishment, and it aims at the long-term well-being even of the offender. Indeed, the aim of punishment is to bring both criminal and victims to a state in which they can live together, relationship restored.

In human affairs, this is often an unattainable ideal. The criminal would have to realize the gravity of the offence, sincerely regret the offence, and seek to make amends in whatever way is possible. The victims would have to be able to accept, at some point, that amends had been made as far as possible, and that the offender really was a renewed person, committed to compassion and positive relationship. Life is often too short for that to happen. But if there is a further existence after death, there would be ample time for offenders to make amends and learn to love again. And the victims will themselves not be able to enter the kingdom of God unless they in turn are prepared to forgive those who have turned from evil and hatred.

This process would seem to require a period, probably a long one (an 'age') in which the offender could come to realize the effects of actions upon others, and could make amends and have a genuine change of heart. The length of time would depend on the offender. A change of heart would always be possible, especially if God stands ready to help and guide. But it might take a long while. Possibly it might never occur, for it may be that some will remain obdurate in their hatreds and self-obsessions – that we cannot know.

Such a state might be called punishment. But it would not be purely retributive. What occurs in that state will be a result of what the person concerned has made of his or her life. There will, to use the main metaphors that Jesus used in parables, be the 'burning fire' of selfish desires, and the 'outer darkness' of a life without love and compassion. But 'I am convinced that neither death nor life, nor angels, nor rulers, nor things present, nor things to come, nor powers, nor height, nor depth, nor anything else in all creation, will be able to separate us from the love of God' (Rom. 8.38–39). That sounds conclusive – God's love will not be ended by death nor by anything at all, so no punishment will be without hope of ending.

Restorative punishment, then, is God's will, and if any do not accept the offer of release it will not be God who so compels them, but their own obdurate wills which refuse all divine help. In this sense, God does not 'send' people to hell. They choose hell, a state in which hatred, malevolence and unbridled passion rule unchecked, for themselves.

When Matthew speaks of 'age-long punishment' (Matt. 25.46), the word translated as 'age-long' or 'eternal' is *aionios*. From this many Christians have concluded that people may suffer torment literally for ever. And they somehow think that it will be a totally loving and just God who will do this.

Is it not more reasonable, however, to think that 'punishment of the age' means 'punishment for the duration of an age' than 'punishment without end'? And what is the duration of an age? Well, we may say that the 'age' of the patriarchs has come to an end, that the 'age' of the new dispensation in Christ has begun, or that the 'age' of this world will be succeeded by a 'new age'. In that case, we might speak of a punishment of this age, the age when the gospel is preached in the earth but the kingdom has not yet fully come. Punishment, in other words, belongs to the time before the dawning of the new creation, to the age of tribulation in which we live.

This may well be a very long time, when we measure it by earthly days and years. But in the afterlife there is no such measure of time. Subjectively, the torment of the damned is an unmeasurable experience, and clock measures of time do not apply. The time of hell is not measurable time; no doubt it fills the consciousness of those who experience it, but time does not pass by the ticking of a clock, as it does in our present space-time.

Of course it will be the same for Paradise. It will not pass by the ticking of a clock. It will be an intensity of joy, as the presence of God illuminates the whole of the consciousness of the saints. There will be no possibility of boredom, for time will not seem to pass or to hang heavy on our hands. There will be no anxiety about when the experience will end, for it will be a consciousness of total ecstasy, with no feeling of transience or loss, in one unbounded present.

It is as measured by the time of this world that hell and Paradise endure as long as our present age endures, and so will be age-long. But a new creation will come, and then this age will end. In that new creation, evil and suffering will be no more, and all those who have not consciously and freely rejected the love of God will rise to life with God. Of any others there may be we cannot speak, but we are told, even in one of the most blood-thirsty books of the Bible, that 'Death and Hades [the Greek translation of *Sheol*] were thrown into the lake of fire. This is the second death' (Rev. 20.14). The second death is the final and complete destruction of those who will not accept a life of love; for in a world of pure love, in the conscious presence of God, there is no longer any place in which they can exist.

Development beyond the Bible: the cosmic story to which the Bible points

As I have shown, it is very misleading to take the Bible as a set of accurate historical records, laws that ought to be literally obeyed, and prophecies about exactly what is going to happen in our human future.

The Bible is a set of human writings, guided by the Spirit of God to form a developing and diverse set of discernments of God in many different historical contexts. Its images can be paths to fuller apprehensions of God as a creator with unbounded love for creation and for humans who are capable of conscious awareness of God, who wills that they should grow in intellectual and moral understanding, and finally come to share in the eternal divine life. But biblical images can also be barriers to understanding, depicting God as a vindictive, nationalistic tyrant, who condemns most of the world's population to endless torment, and lays down laws that are to be obeyed whether or not we can see any point in them.

For Christians, the long story of developing biblical discernments of God is essential for an adequate understanding of the person of Jesus, who was seen by his followers as a prophet, as the foretold Messianic King, and as a High Priest who bridged the gulf between God and estranged humanity by uniting in his own person the self-giving loving invitation of God and the self-offering loving response of perfected humanity. Because of this, the whole biblical record needs to be re-interpreted by Christians in the light of the person of Jesus, and individual passages of the Bible need to be assessed by the ideal of Christ which they anticipate.

As Christians have reflected upon that ideal, their understanding has been further shaped by their common life of prayer and of experienced companionship with the risen Christ. Through two thousand years of history, they have been able to bring new perspectives to bear which give a broader and deeper under-standing of the place of Jesus in God's created cosmos. The New Testament letters give expression to the radically new spiritual life and understanding that the risen Christ brought to them. From the very first, they are not content to simply repeat the story of one historical figure whom many of them had met and known. They seek to place Jesus in the context of cosmic history, as a culminat-ing ideal of God's purpose for creation. Of course, their view of cosmic history was very limited. They placed earth at the centre of their cosmos, and its history was short, only a few thousand years long. In that context, it was natural to see Jesus as having been born in 'the last days' (2 Pet. 3.3). He would return soon, within a generation, in glory, and 'the day of the Lord', the day of the judge-ment upon and elimination of evil from the earth, would come suddenly, like a thief in the night.

Already, however, the writer of the second letter of Peter warned that 'with the Lord one day is like a thousand years' (2 Pet. 3.8), and that God does not want anyone to perish 'but all to come to repentance' (verse 9). As the first generations of Christians consid-ered this, they began to have a greater sense of the size of the earth, of the peoples who had never heard of Christ, and of generations of people who might yet be born. They considered that 'repent-ance and forgiveness of sins is to be proclaimed in his name to all nations' (Luke 24.47). Their horizons expanded, and Paul wrote, probably towards the end of his life, in his letter to the Romans: 'a hardening has come upon part of Israel, until the full number of the Gentiles has come in. And so all Israel will be saved' (Rom. 11.25–26). The 'full number of the Gentiles' has to hear the gospel, and be offered a real chance of salvation – of the knowl-edge and love of God in Jesus Christ. What is that number? No human knows; but it seems clear that it will take thousands of years before the gospel is preached in a clear and compelling way to all nations.

Paul, or some followers of Paul, took this thought even further. The writer of the letter to the Ephesians says that the 'mystery of the divine will', revealed in Christ, is 'a plan for the fullness of time, to gather up all things in him, things in heaven and things on earth' (Eph. 1.10). Admittedly, the cosmos (all things in heaven) was in their opinion pretty small. Still, it was the whole created universe, and all beings (like angels, for instance) who live in that universe. This idea links with the similar idea, in John and in Colossians, that the whole universe was created in Christ ('In him all things in heaven and on earth were created', Col. 1.16). Now Christ is seen as the archetypal pattern of creation, and as the final all-including reality within which all creation will be gathered up and unified.

This is a breath-taking expansion of vision. Within Christian faith from the earliest years was the idea that the 'return of Christ in glory' will not just be some event in the earth's future. It will be the uniting of all creation in that all-embracing reality through which the cosmos was created, the eternal Word. That Word was embodied in Jesus as fully as it could be in the finite human world. But it is a cosmic spiritual reality that contains the potentialities of all created beings, and that is to contain the actualized unity of all such beings, insofar as they have come into being in the history of the cosmos.

If there is a God, then the consciousness of God will contain knowledge of the whole history of the cosmos. That knowledge will not fade or disappear, and so all things will be remembered for ever in God. Yet in the mind of God their character will be changed, as God integrates all things into the total vision of beauty and goodness that is the anticipation and the goal of creation. No suffering will be wholly lost or forgotten. But it will be redeemed in God, as its felt quality is transformed from one of agonizing loss and pain to a less intensely felt fragment of a process which had to be what it was, given the choices that were made and the ends to which it was directed. Pain will be subsumed and suffused by glory and joy in God – somewhat as the memory of pain in a human life can be ameliorated by later recognition of a journey towards a greater fulfilment of which it was a part.

The gospel of the resurrection is that God will not only remember us, and all we have suffered and enjoyed and done. God will raise us to share in that divine awareness of what we have been, so that we will see meaning even in those parts of our lives that seemed most meaningless. We will see how our lives were part of a larger pattern, and how, even while we were lost in a far country and in an estranged world, God was drawing us nearer to the divine life and to a unique purpose and vocation that was ours alone.

Moreover, in that resurrection life we will continue to grow in developing the potentialities God implanted in us in our creation. We will be able to deepen the friendships that were so often muted or abruptly ended in our earthly lives. We will be able to fulfil all the possibilities for unique creativity, friendship and sensitivity that have always been implicit within us. That is why Christians speak of the 'resurrection of the body'. It is not that corpses climb out of earthly tombs. It is that the life of heaven is a fuller life, when all our properly human capacities can find greater realization, and when we can flourish in societies of love as we adventure into the endless life of God.

So 'the end of time' does not happen with some human person dropping down from the clouds on Jerusalem. It is the transfiguration of all creation into the conscious life of God, something that can only be completed when the whole cosmic history has come to an end. The images used in the New Testament are images of an ascent into the clouds. But what they stand for is the raising of human life to the *Shekinah*, the cloud of the glory of the presence of God.

The scope and wonder of this was beyond the imagination of the disciples of Jesus. Their image of a return to earth in clouds of glory was the best they could understand. But implicit in the image was a picture that could only be made explicit centuries later, when the planets and stars could be properly seen as other worlds in a vast expanse of space. And only in the last hundred years has the full extent of our universe become apparent. There are a hundred billion stars in our galaxy, and a hundred billion galaxies in our visible universe, and beyond that there may be realities as yet unknown and in a myriad diverse forms.

Is Christ their pattern and their goal, from which they find their origin and form, and within which they will find a final harmonious and integrated unity, beyond destruction and sorrow? If Christ is indeed identical with the infinite reality of God, then of course the answer is 'yes'. But now it may begin to seem unduly arrogant to view human history as central to the story of the cosmos, or humans as the most important beings in the cosmos. If that is so, it will do us no harm to know it. Why should we regard humans, so late arriving on the cosmic scene, and yet so early in its total history, as the one culmination and purpose of its existence?

The creator's purposes are vaster than we can conceive. They will certainly include the creation of millions of mathematically elegant and beautiful forms of being, which can be created, appreciated and enjoyed for their own sake. As the book of Proverbs puts it, the divine wisdom 'was beside [God] like a little child . . . rejoicing in his inhabited world' (Prov. 8.30–31, NRSV alternative translation). According to some Indian traditions, the cosmos is the *lila*, the play of the Supreme Lord. It is his dance, his artistic self-expression. The cosmos has value even if there are no sentient beings, for it is part of the creative expression of the mind, wisdom and energy of God.

It is surely good, however, if sentient beings come to exist, which can in various ways and degrees share in the knowledge and appreciation of the cosmos. Jewish and Christian tradition holds that such beings are not inserted into the physical universe like passengers in a boat. They are intrinsic parts of the physical universe, developing out of the potentialities of the material cosmos the ability to know and understand, to love and appreciate, to participate in shaping, the future of the physical in its fullest actualization.

So we can see the cosmos generated as a field of immense potentiality, law-like and integrated from its first beginnings, drawn through a process of creative emergence towards innumerable forms of organized complexity. Some of these forms issue in conscious valuing life which, through struggle, endeavour and social self-development, can ascend to fulfilment by sharing in the conscious life of God.

We do not know how many different forms of conscious intelligence there are in our cosmos. Perhaps humans are the only ones, or the first, though that does not seem necessary or important. We do know that in the human world the creative freedom of personal life has led, over many generations, to alienation and estrangement from a sense of the presence of God as supreme beauty, truth and goodness. Our inability to know the good or to do even what we think to be good has compromised human life and corrupted the course of its development.

Within this cosmic picture of the emergence of consciousness and the human fall into estrangement the Christian gospel can be seen more clearly as the sharing of God in the struggle and estrangement of the human world, in order to lead humans to share in the life of God. That is what the death and resurrection of Jesus makes manifest, in the particularities of our human history. Throughout the whole cosmos we can see the emergence of the personal (of consciousness, value and purpose) from the physical (unconscious and impersonal). The physical universe from the Big Bang to the first onset of conscious life is of course of great value to God for its beauty and organized complexity. It is not without value or purpose. Yet when conscious life comes to exist it introduces a new element to creation, an element which eventually becomes capable of conscious relationship to God and participation in the work of God's creative activity – though it also becomes capable of falling into self-centredness and frustration of God's purpose.

We may be sure that God works throughout this process universally to empower the long ascent from the blind interactions of the dust of stars to conscious understanding and love of the good and beautiful. Whether on other planets there is conscious life, and whether that life has fallen into estrangement and self-love, we cannot know. What we do know is that on this small blue planet God has acted to liberate us from the self-centredness which was always a negative possibility for our world, and unite us again to the divine life. And we know that the particular act of God in Christ shows the way in which God will act throughout the whole cosmos, to complete the story of the emergence of its myriad potentialities from its divine origin to its divine goal.

In John's Gospel Jesus says, 'I am the way, and the truth, and the life' (John 14.6). The eternal Word and wisdom of God opens the way from the finite to the infinite for all sentient beings who respond to his call. On this planet, that Word is manifest and expressed in the person of Jesus. Those who become his disciples witness to the self-giving liberating love of God throughout the whole cosmos. In this way the modern scientifically informed view of the universe enormously expands our understanding of who Jesus was. In this sense the biblical witness to Jesus points beyond itself to the ultimate nature of Being as redemptive love.

We still have much to learn of what this implies for our lives and for the life of our planet. The Bible will always remain the central and definitive witness to the character of the love of God, discerned gradually over centuries through the prophets, and culminating in the life, death and resurrection of Jesus. But it is essential that we should see the one to whom the Bible points as the source of our new life in Christ and as the focal point of God's self-revelation to us. The Bible is not a text-book of true facts and doctrines. It is the witness to life-changing discernments of God, which occur as the events of human history are seen in the light of the eternal reality of God. And for Christians it culminates in that event which becomes the clue to the nature of the whole cosmic process, the death and resurrection of Jesus, definitively disclosing the unlimited, self-emptying and transfiguring love of God. If and insofar as the Bible, read in the many communities of the Church, is the vehicle of such a disclosure, then we can say, carefully and sensitively and with discrimination, that it is indeed the definitive resource of Christian faith, the guide of Christian lives, an authoritative library of books inspired by the Spirit of God, and able to evoke in its readers a sense of the presence of God.

Conclusion: the Bible as the word of God

To read the Bible in this way four main things are required. First, we need a sense of history, so that we can see when, in what circumstances, and for whom, its various writings were composed. We need to see its diversity and the developments of thought and understanding that it contains, so that we can place particular texts within the total story of changing human insights into the nature and purposes of God that is found in the Bible as we now have it.

Second, we need a sense of metaphor, to escape from narrowly literalist interpretations and see how imagery is used in the Bible to convey disclosures of God, to speak of that which is beyond all finite reality, and to evoke new and uniquely personal spiritual perceptions in its hearers or readers.

Third, we need to learn from the scholarly work of those who have spent their lives in the study of biblical texts in the original languages. We cannot agree with every scholarly claim, since scholars very often disagree. But we should be aware of these disputes, and of the reasons for them, so that our own view can be free from unjustified certainty and arrogance, and so that we can discriminate between those things to which we should be unconditionally committed in practice and those things where theoretical certainty is unavailable.

Fourth, we need a sense of transcendence, of a spiritual presence that is known in and through many historical, natural and personal facets of experienced being. Without such a sense, the Bible will be only a record of the false beliefs of ancient peoples. With it, the Bible can become a path to awareness of the self-giving God who offers to all humanity the unambiguously good news that all are invited to share in the divine experience of a world redeemed through love.

Approached with a critical mind and an open heart, the Bible can be read as a great spiritual text, pointing beyond itself to the positive gospel of eternal freedom, joy and compassion which was the gospel of Jesus. If there is indeed a God, a spiritual being of wisdom, compassion and joy, who is the origin and underlying reality of the cosmos, then we might hope to find clues to its nature and its purpose in creation somewhere in our history. We might hope that such a cosmic intelligence might communicate these things to us, in part at least. But we might expect that such revelation would be mediated through the limitations and the corruptions of human minds, so that it will always be to some extent ambiguous and allusive.

Among the many human records that point, or claim to point, to such revelations, the Christian Bible witnesses to a long historical tradition of diverse and developing revelations, culminating in the life, death and resurrection of Jesus of Nazareth, which it interprets as a definitive self-revelation of God in our history, and the origin of a way of liberation from selfish desire and union with God through the co-operative inward activity of the Spirit of Christ.

The Christian Bible is the canonical text of the many human communities that follow this spiritual path. Christians believe that God can use its very diverse documents, difficult but rewarding to interpret as they are, to evoke a sense of divine presence and purpose, and to lead its hearers into a closer conscious relationship with the divine mind and heart of Being. To seek to understand the Bible in this way is to understand it as a spiritual text, as, in a carefully qualified sense, the word of God. And that, whether one finally accepts its teaching or not, is what it is intended to be.

Index